Top Notes

Tim Winton's
The Boy Behind the Curtain

Study notes for Common Module:
Texts and Human Experiences
2019–2023 HSC

Bruce Pattinson

A
FIVE SENSES
PUBLICATION

Five Senses Education Pty Ltd
2/195 Prospect Highway
Seven Hills 2147
New South Wales
Australia

Pattinson, Bruce
Top Notes – The Boy Behind the Curtain
ISBN 978-1-76032-234-2

CONTENTS

TOP NOTES SERIES

This series has been created to assist HSC students of English in their understanding of set texts. Top Notes are easy to read, providing analysis of issues and discussion of important ideas contained in the texts.

Particular care has been taken to ensure that students are able to examine each text in the context of the module it has been allocated to.

Each text generally includes:

- Notes on the specific module
- Plot summary
- Character analysis
- Setting
- Thematic concerns
- Language studies
- Essay questions and a modelled response
- Other textual material
- Study practice questions
- Useful quotes

We have covered the areas we feel are important for students in their study of *Texts and Human Experiences* for their Common Module. I am sure you will find these Top Notes useful in your studies of English.

Bruce Pattinson
Series Editor

COMMON MODULE: TEXTS AND HUMAN EXPERIENCES

"It is quite possible—overwhelmingly probable, one might guess— that we will always learn more about human life and personality from novels than from scientific psychology"

NOAM CHOMSKY

What is the Common Module?

The Common Module set for the 2019–23 HSC is *Texts and Human Experiences*. It is compulsory to study this topic as prescribed by NESA and it is common to all three English courses. Remember: you will be learning how texts reveal individual and collective human experiences. There are no right or wrong answers in this module – it is about how you see and interpret material and engage with it.

In the Common Module you will be analysing one prescribed text and a range of short texts that are related to the idea of human experiences. You will analyse texts not only to investigate the ideas they present about this area but also how they convey these ideas. This means you will be looking closely at the techniques a composer uses to represent his / her messages and shape meaning. You will also be looking at relationships between texts in regard to the experiences you explore. Overall, you will become an expert on texts and the human experience — that is, the different notions people have about human experience and the various ways composers manipulate techniques to communicate their ideas about it.

Specifically you will look at one set text from the following list.

- Doerr, Anthony, *All the Light We Cannot See*
- Lohrey, Amanda, *Vertigo*
- Orwell, George, *Nineteen Eighty-Four*
- Parrett, Favel, *Past the Shallows*
- Dobson, Rosemary 'Young Girl at a Window', 'Over the Hill', 'Summer's End', 'The Conversation', 'Cock Crow', 'Amy Caroline', 'Canberra Morning'
- Slessor, Kenneth 'Wild Grapes', 'Gulliver', 'Out of Time', 'Vesper-Song of the Reverend Samuel Marsden', 'William Street', 'Beach Burial'
- Harrison, Jane, *Rainbow's End*
- Miller, Arthur, *The Crucible*
- Shakespeare, William, *The Merchant of Venice*
- Winton, Tim, *The Boy Behind the Curtain* Chapters: 'Havoc: A Life in Accidents', 'Betsy', 'Twice on Sundays', 'The Wait and the Flow', 'In the Shadow of the Hospital', 'The Demon Shark', 'Barefoot in the Temple of Art'
- Yousafzai, Malala & Lamb, Christina, *I am Malala*
- Daldry, Stephen, *Billy Elliot*
- O'Mahoney, Ivan, *Go Back to Where You Came From –* Series 1, Episodes 1, 2 and 3 and *The Response*
- Walker, Lucy, *Waste Land*

NESA has mandated that students must study a related text as part of the common module, and that this should be part of their in-school assessment. However there is NO LONGER a requirement to write about a related text in the HSC examination itself.

WHAT DOES NESA REQUIRE FOR THE COMMON MODULE?

The NESA documentation of the Common Module: Texts and Human Experiences states that students:

- deepen their understanding of how texts represent individual and collective human experiences;

- examine how texts represent human qualities and emotions associated with, or arising from, these experiences;

- appreciate, explore, interpret, analyse and evaluate the ways language is used to shape these representations in a range of texts in a variety of forms, modes and media;

- explore how texts may give insight into the anomalies, paradoxes and inconsistencies in human behaviour and motivations, inviting the responder to see the world differently, to challenge assumptions, ignite new ideas or reflect personally;

- may also consider the role of storytelling throughout time to express and reflect particular lives and cultures;

- by responding to a range of texts, further develop skills and confidence using various literary devices, language concepts, modes and media to formulate a considered response to texts;

- study one prescribed text and a range of short texts that provide rich opportunities to further explore representations of human experiences illuminated in texts;

- make increasingly informed judgements about how aspects of these texts, for example, context, purpose, structure, stylistic and grammatical features, and form shape meaning;

- select one related text and draw from personal experience to make connections between themselves, the world of the text and their wider world;

- by responding and composing throughout the module, further develop a repertoire of skills in comprehending, interpreting and analysing complex texts;

- examine how different modes and media use visual, verbal and/or digital language elements;

- communicate ideas using figurative language to express universal themes and evaluative language to make informed judgements about texts;

- further develop skills in using metalanguage, correct grammar and syntax to analyse language and express a personal perspective about a text

If this is what is required by NESA, we need to examine the concept of human experience carefully so we can adequately respond in these ways. I would recommend that you read the complete document which is on the NESA web site and can be downloaded in Word or Adobe. Understanding this document is an important step in handling the textual material within the guidelines required — remember you are reading for a purpose and should make notes and highlight ideas as you read so that you can develop these ideas later.

UNDERSTANDING THE COMMON MODULE

What are Human Experiences?

The concept of Human Experiences is at the heart of the Common Module.

Human Experiences are experiences of individuals or a group of people (eg a family, society, or nation) in life. There are a very wide range of human experiences which include but go beyond this list:

- feelings or reactions (momentary or long term): love, hate, anger, joy, fear, disgust
- key milestones or stages: birth, childhood, adulthood, marriage, divorce, death
- culture, belonging and identity
- conformity and rebellion
- innocence and guilt, justice
- freedom and repression
- education, vocation, work, sport, leisure
- attraction to a person, idea, group or cause
- opposition to an idea, cause, political system
- religious faith or belief
- extreme events such as an earthquake, avalanche, tsuanami
- regular events such as walking, eating, singing, dancing, discussing ideas.

The word *experience* seems innately connected to the human condition and it is something we have each day whether a mundane experience that is repetitive, or something new and dramatic which offers challenges and rewards. Experiences can vary greatly in their impact on individuals, groups and countries. One example might be a war that is a negative experience for a whole population while we may experience the wonder of medicine with a new vaccine for a deadly disease that saves millions of people. We need to note that the module asks for 'experiences' ...we are a combination of different experiences and each has a varying impact. One person's problem is another's challenge depending on perspective, skill set, previous experience and ability.

Experiences are widespread and often shared: this is why people tell their stories and these shared experiences form part of our cultural heritage. These experiences often inform, warn and teach across entire cultural groups and many stories are shared across cultures.

DEFINING HUMAN EXPERIENCES

Now let's attempt to define what human experiences are and shape them into a more coherent and easily understood framework so we can begin our investigation at a basic level of understanding before moving into more complex analysis and looking at how the texts illuminate our understanding of the term.

Dictionary.com defines the term **experience** as:

noun

1. a particular instance of personally encountering or undergoing something:

2. the process or fact of personally observing, encountering, or undergoing something:

3. the observing, encountering, or undergoing of things generally as they occur in the course of time:
   to learn from experience; the range of human experience.

4. knowledge or practical wisdom gained from what one has observed, encountered, or undergone, e.g. *a man of experience.*

5. *Philosophy.* the totality of the cognitions given by perception; all that is perceived, understood, and remembered.

verb

(used with object), **experienced, experiencing.**

6. to have experience of; meet with; undergo; feel, e.g. *to experience nausea.*

7. to learn by experience.

idiom

8. **experience religion**, to undergo a spiritual conversion by which one gains or regains faith in God.

Obviously there are a number of definitions according to context, but all are applicable to our study in some shape or form, as the range of human experience is so vast. The search for 'new experience' has driven much of the development of people, groups, cultures and nations over past millennia. New experiences are always met with excitement and often trepidation as to what change they might bring.

Think historically about how people have reacted to change. It can cause great upheavals in society, with violent reactions while other changes brought through various experiences are welcomed and may change how people live and comprehend the world. Experiences affect us emotionally in many cases rather than logically and when we respond emotionally, behaviours become unpredictable. This causes the paradoxes, anomalies and inconsistencies mentioned in the rubric. If we were logical beings the world would be an easier place, but probably more boring.

These definitions all point to the fact that memory is the key to experience. The experience is stored in memory and drawn upon when the circumstances are repeated or closely mimicked so we can deal with them — hopefully better than on the initial experience.

Experiences can come in many ways and the synonyms listed below for experience help us to understand the concept even further. They assist in defining how an experience can arise:

Synonyms

actions	understanding	judgment
background	wisdom	observation
contacts	acquaintances	perspicacity
involvement	actuality	practicality
know-how	caution	proofs
maturity	combat	savoir-faire
participation	doings	seasonings
patience	empiricism	sophistication
practice	evidence	strife
reality	existences	trials
sense	exposures	worldliness
skill	familiarity	forebearance
struggle	intimacy	
training	inwardness	

http://www.thesaurus.com/browse/experience?s=t

These synonyms show partly the vast array of words that our language has created around this concept, and also shows how important it is in the human psyche. We, as humans, want to experience. Now we will look at some examples of experiences and examine how they can have an impact. It is also important to remember that experiences do not have to be positive. You might experience a huge problem, a bereavement, a car accident, an unwelcome relationship or something totally bizarre that rocks your world. There can be a more opaque side to any experience that may need to be addressed.

The whole aim of this Common Module is to examine the text closely but also relate it to the concept of human experiences and decide how examining it in this way enables us to better understand both the text and the concept of humanity.

It is important that you unpack what each text you study shows you about human experiences and what ideas / themes arise from those experiences. Formulate your own ideas about the text.

Read the NESA Stage 6 document called *English Stage 6: Annotations of selected texts prescribed for the Higher School Certificate 2019-23* (see *www.educationstandards.nsw.edu.au*) for the set text you are studying. This document offers insights into the way each particular text should be examined by outlining key ideas and areas for clarification.

Human experiences and ways of experiencing vary due to individual circumstance and these experiences can change many things about individual lives, communities and the world. When we examine the concept of human experience in relation to a text, we need to examine the assumptions or biases we bring to it as well as how experiencing the text itself may change us and how we view things. The text may challenge and confront how we view the human experience or we may have preconceived ideas that make it more difficult for this to happen.

Students can also think about their own 'personal experience to make connections between themselves, the world of the text and their wider world.' Examining and enjoying any text is an experience in itself but it is what we take away from the text and apply that is the crucial aspect. That is not to say that every text will be enjoyed or offer a human experience that is significant either positively or negatively. Some texts may not personally engage you and that is fine. This is especially so when you begin to look for other related material that links to *Texts and Human Experiences*. We recommend that you find examples of texts that link but also personally appeal to you so that you can relate empathetically with them.

Individual Human Experiences

The idea of personal experiences is a popular and pervasive concept, especially in the literature of many cultures. Recording personal experiences as a means of sharing wisdom or more mundane daily tasks is part of human nature and we record and relate these experiences frequently. Experiences are recorded and relayed in many ways. We tell oral stories in both anecdotal and formal ways, we write, draw, sing and photograph our way into history (or not). Look at the proliferation of social media in this current century as people record their daily, even hourly, experiences for all to see. We record the most trivial details of our lives for likes and followers while the real world passes us by. Human experiences affect us on a daily basis and some experiences influence our lives and the way we live them.

Individuals seek out experiences in a variety of ways. Some seek more and more extreme experiences to test themselves against the world. Others limit their experiences. A lot of people prefer the familiar and don't actively seek new experiences. Individuals, it must be remembered, also see experiences in different ways and the same experience may have a very different impact on individuals. The one thing we can be certain about is that experiences are part of humanity and even the most limited of us have them. Many of these experiences also come from interaction with others and as noted we also like to share these experiences.

Experiences are what define us in many ways and are what makes us human.

We are going to look at four specific ways that experiences can influence us as people over the next few pages. These are physical, psychological, emotional and intellectual experiences and many experiences are a combination of these.

Physical Experience

The concept of a physical experience is tied into the human experience and part of the collective experience as well. Individuals seek physical experiences to test themselves against nature and other individuals often as part of trials and rituals, for example being integrated into a community. In modern times individuals have sought to test themselves with extreme sports and explorations into the harshest conditions and even space. Physical experiences can also change the way we see the world and others because of the chemical changes these experiences have on our bodies and mind. Physical experiences are often challenges and part of the experience is overcoming adversity. These physical challenges are often celebrated, as in the case of sports, but can also offer challenges if the experience is a negative one such as an accident or disease. Physical experiences are also often quite public and thus have permeated our societies in both their execution and how they are perceived. These physical experiences, even if experienced vicariously, have become popular across cultures and celebrated. Think of examples for yourself but most competitive sports offer examples.

Bruce Lee extends the concept of the physical experience into all aspects of life and that's what we will look at next in our analysis of human experiences –

'If you always put limits on everything you do, physical or anything else, it will spread into your work and into your life. There are no limits. There are only plateaus, and you must not stay there, you must go beyond them.'

Psychological Experience

The idea of a psychological experience is tied into many of the abstract ideas that people experience and can lead to a discussion of what is normal psychology. From the earliest times humans have attempted to alter their psychology through a number of experiences. On a simple level this can be a drug that changes the person's or group's perspective on reality. Examples of this might be alcohol or marijuana but cultural groups also use various substances to share group experiences. This can be seen in Native American cultures with *peyote*. In more modern times prescription drugs that are mood altering have been used to minimise the symptoms of psychiatric illnesses such as depression, and these mood altering drugs are common and legal. Others attempt to alter their psychology by seeing specialists in this area while others act out their condition leading to social and criminal issues. When discussing the human experience, psychology is a key issue and will form a part of most studies of experience. When taken too far this search for a new psychological experience can be harmful eg. an addiction.

Carl Jung, the famous psychologist, comments on the problems of addiction for human experiences, stating clearly that excess can be an issue:

"Every form of addiction is bad, no matter whether the narcotic be alcohol, morphine or idealism."

Emotional Experience

According to the psychologist, Robert Plutchik, there are eight basic emotions:

- **Fear** — feeling afraid.
- **Anger** — feeling angry. A stronger word for anger is rage.
- **Sadness** — feeling sad. Other words are sorrow, grief (a stronger feeling, for example when someone has died) or **depression** (feeling sad for a long time without any external cause). Some people think depression is a different emotion.
- **Joy** — feeling happy. Other words are happiness, gladness.
- **Disgust** — feeling something is wrong or nasty
- **Trust** — a positive emotion; admiration is stronger; **acceptance** is weaker
- **Anticipation** — in the sense of looking forward positively to something which is going to happen. **Expectation** is more neutral; **dread** is more negative.

https://simple.wikipedia.org/wiki/List_of_emotions

Emotions are the strongest drivers of human experience and form lasting aspects of any experience. Think about breaking up with someone you love and the emotions that drive behaviours in this situation. People have all sorts of extreme behaviours under the influence of emotions and these experiences are often the ones recorded and those which influence us most. Think about the role emotions play in our lives and the range of emotions from the list above. Consider how much emotions affect our life experiences, how they influence our decisions which decide our experiences and on a higher level consider how they affect the decisions which may seriously impact our experiences, such as politicians going to war.

Intellectual Experience

The concept of an intellectual experience is linked to decisions and experiences we have based on analysis and logic rather than the emotional choices referred to in the previous section. These intellectual experiences have changed the way we live and how we have seen our world. These experiences have affected the way we as humans have altered our world to suit our needs and lead to all the great advances in human society and thus experiences. Changes in our ideas, beliefs etc. alter the way we interact with the world and often these intellectual changes come at great cost.

Think of the time in Europe when the Church dominated and stopped scientific advances by calling them heresy/witchcraft. Open societies are more open to new ideas and this is what has hastened the pace of intellectual experiences as dominant ideologies fall away. Intellectual advances may not have the excitement that the other types produce but perhaps they have a more lasting impact on people, societies and the world in general. Ideas are powerful experiences and people hold beliefs strongly.

Immanuel Kant stated that:

> *"experience without theory is blind, but theory without experience is mere intellectual play."*

Consider this statement in the light of what we have learnt about human experiences. Are they a combination of many factors or can we isolate experiences into simple forms?

What exactly is a human experience?

The titular question reminds us of the old brainteaser: "If a tree falls in a forest and no one is around to hear it, does it make a sound?"

There are two classic responses to this. The more Platonically-minded would say the tree always makes a sound when it falls in the forest. We don't have to be there to hear it; we can imagine the sound of a tree falling in the forest, based on memory of such an event or on the recording of such an event. We know that sound is just vibrating air, and it's safe to say that air always vibrates in response to a tree falling, or a bear growling, or a cicada singing, whether we are there to hear it or not.

The second answer is a more post-structuralist response: the sound doesn't occur on its own; it needs a human ear to be heard. Therefore, if there is no human in the forest to hear the tree fall, then there is no sound. This automatically implies that "experience" of anything requires the presence of a human being, which means there is no such thing as an experience that *isn't* human.

Animal rights activists – or anyone with a beloved pet – would almost certainly reject this notion because it prioritises humans and relegates all other species to a lower class of being: an attitude that most would agree has gotten the human race into an awful lot of environmental trouble over the last 200 years of industrialisation.

In his article (*What is an Experience?*), my learned colleague Paul Hartley describes experience in its most basic form, as "the perception of something else" and "ultimately information about what we have perceived." But does this make it particularly human? Dogs and cats perceive things. Insects perceive things. You could even say that plants perceive things, such as the direction from which the sun is shining. Perception is the most basic of life's survival tools for all manner of flora and fauna.

In her brief but cogent disquisition on the subject (*What is Human?*), another of my learned colleagues, Nadine Hare, asserts that to be human is a social construct. Hartley builds on that notion by suggesting that culture affects experience when we start to share it, because "the words, associations, and priorities we attach to the shared experience define how we understand the world we live in."

Hare rightly points out that this world is increasingly dominated by consumerism, which has distorted what it means to be human by excluding all of the attributes and qualities that "make people people." Calling us consumers reduces our experiences to mere transactions. It defines human experience within the narrow confines of the purchase funnel and has little interest in anything that isn't a purchase driver.

Perhaps the field of commerce is where the experiential rubber most emphatically meets the road. Unlike mere perception, commerce is a uniquely human experience. It has mediated, automated, and dominated the human agenda to the point where we are defined by what we buy and little else. Commerce has invaded the non-profit spheres of government, health, and education, imposing its own priorities and principles on these institutions in the expectation that they will behave more like businesses. And even though business still strives to appeal to the so-called masses, it prioritises the pursuit of individual wealth, and in so doing, not only inhibits the desire for shared experience but unravels the social fabric historically woven by the democratic tradition.

As if in response, that social fabric is being re-woven by our networks. As Hare asserts, "humans both produce technology and are produced through technology." Experience is shared more now than it ever has been because the experiential platform – i.e., that very human invention called the internet – is in place to facilitate it like never before, and on a global scale.

This sharing capability reintroduces all of those things that "make people people" back into the conversation – whether commercial or political. What "makes people people" is messy, unpredictable, emotional, and complex. Most of what makes us human has no place in the experiential confines of the purchase funnel, and defies any of our attempts to place it there.

The challenge for us as a species is to embrace this new capacity for sharing to keep the agendas of our hegemonic institutions – whether commercial or political – from defining what makes an experience human. A post-consumer business strategy might be one that, as Hare hopes, will "expand our view of people to include the complex and dynamic social, cultural, gendered, spiritual and racialised beings that they are." Maybe then will our shared human experience truly become, as Hartley asserts, the glue that holds us all together as human beings.

Will Novosedlik
MISC magazine

https://miscmagazine.com/what-is-a-human-experience/

This article appeared in the September 2014 edition of MISC magazine. Can you relate to what the article says about human experiences? Do human experiences depend on perception? Does the experience of anything require the presence of a human as experiencer (para 3)? Can the ideas of experience be extended to include perception by plants or animals? Hartley's idea is that "shared human experience" is "the glue that holds us all together as human beings". Is this an oversimplification?

The Impact of Human Experiences

Human experiences have impacts on many levels. On an individual level, we can have changes in our assumptions about the world and people around us; we can ingest new ideas and have these open new vistas of productivity and performance. We can also reflect and build on these experiences to ensure that they are even more meaningful to our lives. Behaviours towards others and the way we respond to the world can manifest themselves in new and different responses. An example might be that through adverse experiences we can build resilience so that the next negative experience isn't as traumatic and we accept it for what it is. Experiences also teach us new behaviours on a very physical level — if you burn yourself once on a flame you learn not to do it again (hopefully).

The impact of human experiences can also be shared in groups and societies. Firstly, let's examine some group dynamics that can be affected by human experiences. Groups share experiences and adapt and develop behaviours that impact on the group as a whole. Think about the notorious 'bonding' sessions sporting teams have that unite them in a common goal. Think about the behaviours of various gangs in our society. We see plenty of examples of this on American television where gangs based on ethnicity and social groupings form specific sets of behaviours that impact on how they interact with each other and the world. These groupings carry assumptions about how they see the world and respond to it. For example, they may have generally negative reactions to law enforcement and this is ingrained into their codes of behaviour. They are suspicious of the world and the people in it — dividing them up into threats, the law and victims. These behaviours are often reinforced by group experiences such as the initiation rituals which are integral to membership.

Often the impact of these behaviours is to perpetuate stereotypes that then categorise the individuals within these groups. The graphic I have included here shows a stereotypical gang member with the suspicious gaze, ubiquitous hoody and scruffy look. These stereotypes reject new ideas and maintain assumptions about the world, often to the detriment of their members. The experiences they have reinforce their own stereotypical way of viewing anything outside the safety of the group and the cycle continues. Of course, other groups have more positive impacts and see the world as a very different place and their experiences are designed to be positive interactions. Think about groups such as Rotary who are constructive in the community. Other groups have specialty interests such as Animal Welfare, Surf Lifesaving and charities.

Normal social interactions impact groups and individuals, but it takes a major event to alter the behaviours of whole societies, especially so in the modern world where societies are large in scale. Earlier in human history smaller experiences could alter the behaviour of societies as they were insignificant in size compared to modern ones. We often fail to remember that many of these ancient societies' behaviours were impacted by superstition, religions and cultural habituation. The modern society as we know it is only a recent phenomenon. Just a few hundred years ago with church rule people were forced to think in a specific

way and punished for not adhering to a theological culture. Think of the Spanish Inquisition, the imprisonment of Galileo and other such restrictions on freedom of thought; scientific breakthroughs were hidden or declared witchcraft. Even recently the world has seen societies kept repressed by failed ideologies. The brutality of such regimes has left deep scars on the social psyche of nations as they try to recover. This has had an impact on the human experiences of whole populations, and societies respond accordingly.

One example might be at the conclusion of the Communist regime in East Germany when the Berlin Wall was destroyed as a visual symbol of the new-found freedom of a whole population of people who had been repressed for decades by a brutal and ever-present regime. Many citizens who had grown up in this system, where you could 'disappear' without trial or real evidence, found the idea that you could express yourself incredible. Many of the

East Germans couldn't believe that this freedom was real and that the Stasi (the secret police) were gone.

Other experiences can affect societies in extreme ways. Think about wars and the impact they have on civilian populations.

Climatic events such as earthquakes change the way that people behave and respond to situations. Catastrophic flooding occurred in the US city of New Orleans in 2005. The US President's response to help was not immediate and the national administration was severely criticised for lack of effective action.

Societies also respond to perceived problems such as pollution. In 1989 the oil tanker Exxon Valdez ran aground in Prince William Sound, Alaska with disastrous results. The effects of this event are still being experienced thirty years later.

Societies can be divided, as we saw with the election of Donald Trump in the United States of America and the reaction of the Political Left.

The impact of human experiences on societies can be quite dramatic, as we have seen, while other experiences (such as an election) can go by without a murmur from societies, no matter who wins. As a last thought before we move on you should also consider the impact of the media on societies in the modern world, and how they influence individuals, societies and the development of ideas.

Problems With Human Behaviour

So far, we have discussed the impact of human experiences on behaviour. Now we can begin to develop some more complex judgements and understandings about the impact of those experiences on human behaviours. In simplistic terms it could be assessed as:

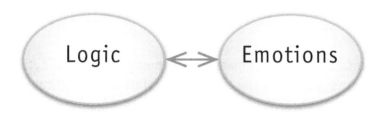

These two opposites on the continuum certainly shape the manner in which we see incidents and how they affect the experience. For instance, if someone you love has no interest in you, it creates a very different reaction to someone you don't care about having no interest in you. It is generally agreed that humans respond more strongly with emotion than they do with logic. Often, it is only through time and reflection that we can understand how an experience has changed and/or altered the manner in which we see a situation or individual.

The Role of Storytelling in Human Experiences

Storytelling has been part of the human experience since 'people' began communicating and it is a method used to convey information and experience as well as be entertaining. Earliest myths were all oral and then people began to write down stories so they weren't lost in time. From this, various theories have developed around storytelling and one is the 'monomyth', which is a template across cultures for storytelling. Let's have a look at this below.

'In narratology and comparative mythology, the monomyth, or the hero's journey, is the common template of a broad category of tales that involve a hero who goes on an adventure, and in a decisive crisis wins a victory, and then comes home changed or transformed.

The concept was introduced in *The Hero with a Thousand Faces* (1949) by Joseph Campbell, who described the basic narrative pattern as follows:

"A hero ventures forth from the world of common day into a region of supernatural wonder: fabulous forces are there encountered and a decisive victory is won: the hero comes back from this mysterious adventure with the power to bestow boons on his fellow man."

Campbell and other scholars, such as Erich Neumann, describe narratives of Gautama Buddha, Moses, and Christ in terms of the monomyth. Critics argue that the concept is too broad or general to be of much use in comparative mythology. Others say that the hero's journey is only a part of the monomyth; the other part is a sort of different form, or colour, of the hero's journey.

https://en.wikipedia.org/wiki/Hero%27s_journey

Storytelling in History and its Purpose in Human Experience

Storytelling in oral form was accompanied by some theatrics to make the stories as entertaining as possible. Many of the early narratives were based upon religious ceremonies and stories of the creation of the earth and people(s). As time moved on, these stories were accompanied by dance, music and/or theatre and often were part of lengthy rituals, often taking days. These stories were designed to bring meaning to people's lives by explaining their own existence and the purpose/meaning of life in a time when life expectancy was short and entertainment was scarce. Of course stories were also recorded as these experiences were significant to all people and these stories run across all cultures. Before writing, stories were recorded in pictures such as cave art, in tattoo designs on skin and in designs such as rock piles and the giant carved heads of Easter Island.

Writing changed the manner in which stories were told and many of the old oral traditions were lost, barely being kept alive by specialists. Stories began to travel across cultural and national boundaries on whatever surface could be created. Papyrus, bones, pottery, skins, paper and in more modern times film, video and digital storage have changed, over time, the way in which stories of human experience have been told and shared. Content evolved from myth, fable and legend to history, personal narratives and commentary. Modern narrative form often has an educational or didactic element and can drift into propaganda. Stories of self-revelation can be instructive and give audiences the opportunity to apply learning to individual lives, whereas historically narrative was used in this way for societies and groups as a whole. In recent times narratives have become interactive and audiences can choose how the narrative unfolds.

Whatever form the story takes we all have a seemingly innate need for narratives to make sense of our lives. They either confirm our world view or alter our world view depending on the experience they convey and the experiences that we bring to the narrative. We need to remember that narratives are important to human experience and have been significant since the beginning of time.

The Text as an Experience

The concept of the text as an experience is one area to consider as we look at *Texts and Human Experiences*. Reading or viewing the text is an experience in itself and when we do this we bring our own history (experiences) to the text and this helps shape our understanding.

Think about the personal perspective that you bring to a text. What are some of your experiences that might influence how you read a particular text? Some texts, especially personal narratives of trial and tribulation or loss, can be confronting to some audiences and bring back strong opinions or emotions. Many texts attempt to do this as they convey a particular point of view about the world.

Does what you bring to the text affect what you learn from that text? We also need to delve into how the narrative experience is conveyed and how this in turn impacts upon the manner in which the story is received by audiences across different cultures. For example, Western films where heroes fight Islamic terrorism may well be viewed very differently by audiences in Western democracies and Islamic countries. Even seemingly innocuous narratives like the movie 'The Red Pill' which is about men's rights and created by a woman, has caused a polarisation of views wherever it has been shown. Strong personal experiences and viewpoints certainly bring their own understandings to texts.

Questions for Texts and Human Experiences

- Define the module in your own words.
- How are people connected by shared experiences?
- How might physical experience(s) change the way you respond to the world?
- How do you think a person's context and prior experiences shape how they perceive the world?
- Are experiences unique or do prior experiences have an impact on a current experience and way of seeing life?
- What is positive about human experiences?
- Discuss what is negative about human experiences.
- To what extent does experience shape the way we see other people and / or groups?
- Is an individual's culture part of their experience or is it something else?
- Is it possible not to have any meaningful experiences at all?
- Why do people tell stories?
- What do you think you might learn from a narrative?

STUDYING A NON-FICTION TEXT

A Non-Fiction text is one where the characters are real people and the events in the story really happened.

If you have ever lived through a set of events or experienced a group of people and tried to write about them, you will know that everyone who experiences something will have his or her own perspective or interpretation of what happened and why. Therefore, non-fiction writing is often very personal. It is seldom simply a matter of relating a set of fixed facts about the situation or the people involved.

The issue of interpretation of a set of events is particularly pertinent to your study of *The Boy Behind the Curtain*, as it usually is in the case of non-fiction writing. You should analyse the features of *The Boy Behind the Curtain* and articulate its interpretation of the events, its attitude to those who participated and its effect on participants and the family as a whole. You should also do this in a critical way – is the interpretation a valid one? You might also want to think about Winton's purpose in writing this text.

The main thing to comprehend, though, is that a non-fiction text is still a text and has *most* things in common with a fiction text. The characters, even though they are real people, are still conjured on the page by the author's language, just as 'made-up' fiction characters are. The structure is determined by the author, or editor, with the intention of telling the story in order to have a certain effect on the reader. This is also as it is in a fiction text.

As well as this, *The Boy Behind the Curtain* is a particular kind of non-fiction text. Not only are the events and 'characters' in the text real people, but the language of the stories is, itself, authentic. In other words, the events, words and the dialogue were composed from real events.

When you are writing about a non-fiction text, you need quotes to substantiate your points, just as with fiction.

It may surprise you to hear that non-fiction outsells fiction in Australia by about four to one. So the analysis and critical reading of non-fiction texts is relevant to the reading habits of Australians.

We also have to consider the autobiographical features of the text. Autobiography is defined in the Oxford Dictionary as 'one's life written by oneself'. An autobiography is a personal recount of a life or events in a life and it generally has a reflective tone. Because it is personal the texts usually reflect the 'self' of the individual.

Autobiography is a popular form of writing as it gives the individual full control over what aspects of their life that they share with the audience. This can lead to omissions or situations where an impartial perspective may have helped. There can often be political and/or emotional bias.

The benefits of the autobiography are that they reflect the feelings and impressions of the author and often convey emotions that are otherwise lost. Autobiography is also a product of its time and autobiography written in reflection is often different with those written in the immediacy of the situation. They may also reflect the political and social mores of the time. For more on the different aspects of autobiography go to:

https://en.wikipedia.org/wiki/Autobiography
https://www.vocabulary.com/dictionary/autobiography

© Five Senses Education Pty Ltd

THE AUTHOR

Tim Winton was born in Perth in 1960. He is the author of fourteen books, ranging from novels, non-fiction, short stories and books for children. He began writing when he was very young and his first novel, *An Open Swimmer,* won the Australian Vogel Prize in 1981.

His classic novel, *Cloudstreet* was published in 1991, winning the Miles Franklin Award that year. It was written mostly in France, suggesting that the author had to distance himself from Australia in order to write the quintessentially Australian novel. It is based on events in the lives of his own family, especially his grandparents and parents. You might note that the novel is dedicated to Winton's grandparents and we read more about them in this text, learning specifics that enlighten us about both family and Australia in the past.

In 2003, the Australian Society of Authors compiled a list of the forty most popular Australian books of all time. There were three Winton novels in the list and *Cloudstreet* was rated first. When asked about this, Tim Winton replied with typical off-hand modesty: 'It's nice to be recognised by your peers, but I don't know if I'd be taking it as gospel.' His work is highly regarded across the globe and his contribution to Australian literature is unquestioned.

As we will read in *The Boy Behind the Curtain*, Winton grew up in the suburbs of Perth in Western Australia. Winton has a love of the Australian landscape and this shows in his prose when he describes where he was raised. He has described his characters as 'figures in landscape', indicating how important setting is in his novels. Many of his characters are searching for the place where they belong. He has acknowledged that his characters become real to him – 'years later you'll have dreams about them.' Perhaps this non-fiction work is his way of searching for his own place – it may be an idea worth considering as we look for examples of human experiences in the text.

More recent novels *The Riders* and *Dirt Music* were both short-listed for the international Booker Prize. Winton's writing is loved for its warmth, humour and perceived characteristic 'Australianness'. He is almost certainly Australia's best-loved novelist.

Tim Winton lives in Western Australia with his wife and three children. He has a down-to-earth image and wears his hair in a long ponytail. He still loves to fish and surf. This text gives us an additional insight into Winton's life and context.

SUMMARY WITH COMMENTARY

Havoc: A Life in Accidents

I

Winton here recreates a specific childhood incident from a time when he was nine years of age. He is in the front seat of the car minding the lantern they used for fishing. His own father's accident is foreshadowed for the reader with the 'personal scent was a cocktail of Dencorub and Quick-Eze'. A motorbike overtakes them at speed and his policeman father whistles as the bike roars past; he has a 'complicated' view of speed.

They see the taillight of the bike disappear and his father comes to a dramatic halt. Winton peers out to see his father tend to the fallen man, move the bike off the road and then calmly drive off to access a phone. After this they return to the crash site and the rider is 'convulsing'. Winton gets the job of stamping on the brake so the ambulance 'could see the lights from a distance'. He knows now it was only a tactic to keep him 'out of harm's way'.

The injured rider is in a bad way with a face like 'raw meat' and 'glossy with blood'. The ambulance arrives and the injured man panics and wants to fight. The scene becomes more complicated when the injured riders drunken father appears and goes 'crazy'. Winton feels a 'treacherous panic' and has 'had no experience of the violence' he sees as the man attacks his unconcerned father. The police come and the 'scene quickly resolved itself'. Back at home his father minimises the incident but the lack of control he felt haunts Winton. It takes him years to work out why he felt this way and eventually he realises it was because his father 'had been taken away...before.'

Winton had adapted to his father's injuries – the scar on his neck and the divots in his hip. He is used to the smell of Dencorub which relieves his father's chronic back pain. The Quick-Eze for the ulcer his anti-inflammatory drugs caused. He cannot take these any more. The accident three years earlier is a part of 'havoc's vanguard' by which he marks parts of life.

II

Despite both his parents wanting a 'predictable and nurturing' environment the family still lived 'in the shadow of havoc'. His father was in 'Accidents' as a job in the police force. He rode a motorbike and was 'oblique' about his work. Part of the job was going to 'fatals' and he was often upset. Winton sees his father become 'guarded, sceptical' and he writes how he 'brought havoc home' despite all his good intentions. When Winton is five 'real trouble' comes in the shape of his father's accident.

A driver fails to stop and slams his father into a brick wall. He suffers profound injuries resulting in a coma. They were told he would never be 'himself' and no one had any great hopes for his recovery. The house is heavy and seemingly without hope, even when he is brought home from hospital. Winton is 'enraged' that a stranger had done this to them and that they were 'no longer the safe, confident people' of before.

Winton finds the helmet his dad had been wearing at the time of the accident and finds it 'flimsy'. He tells of how his father's convalescence had a 'lasting impact' on him and he grew up quickly. His father had to be bathed in bed as he was too heavy to lift but one day; 'unannounced' a stranger turns up and offers to bathe his father. The man brings 'a new energy' to things and gets

his father to the bath but Winton watches him carefully. From the man Winton learns 'something new' about strangers – they can be negative or bring 'mysterious kindness'.

In autumn his father begins to recover quickly and we learn the man 'laid hands' and anointed his father with oil. Both Winton's parents become Christians after this. This change certainly affected Winton and he considers it an 'act of grace'.

III

The 'old man' returns to work and is grateful he can't remember his own accident. Eventually he gets back on his bike and resumes normal duties leaving Winton feeling 'safe again'. He tells how major events like this affect a child's 'sense of self' and he recalls a story he wrote about the bike crash where the child is the hero. He likes 'family life'.

IV

Winton's own accident was close to the motorbike accident he has seen at nine. He is now eighteen and is a passenger in a car that goes through a brick wall. The driver is uninjured but Winton is badly hurt and his mother faints watching him have seizures in the hospital. He goes through his own convalescence at home where he is 'feeble and mentally stuck and now sees it as depression. However the weeks in bed made him concentrate on being a writer. 'Havoc' had forced him into focussing on writing and his injuries won't ever allow him to do a physical job so he has no fall back. He had to write and do it well.

V

Winton in this section tells us how he liked to flirt with death as a teenager. He dived into caves where it was 'claustrophobic and dangerous' without oxygen and this made him 'feel alive' he doesn't have the need for this anymore as some of his friends do. He finds you become attuned to havoc and know when it begins. These moments 'can come and go' and he recalls an accident where he helped and despite a 'happy outcome' he was 'a fucking mess'. It's times like this that you find self.

VI

Winton, being 'a copper's son' has an eye for trouble and he loves routine. While some people think they have 'domesticated chaos' they cannot cope with any disruption and truly prefer 'predictability'. Winton thinks we will always 'be vulnerable to havoc' and nothing can stop it. His father 'survived a career in havoc'. Havoc, Winton points out is the stuff of writing and we know it is coming but not how it ends.

Questions for 'Havoc: A Life in Accidents'

1. Define the word 'havoc' in your own words.

2. Winton comments on THREE accidents in 'Havoc: A Life in Accidents'. What are the three accidents and how did ONE affect him psychologically?

3. List five things we learn about Winton from reading this story.

4. How does information about his family situation make Winton seem more 'human' rather than a reclusive writer?

5. Think here about the use of personal anecdote. What is the impact of an anecdote and why are they effective in conveying ideas to the audience?

6. Why do Winton's parents become Christians? Did you find this whole scenario unusual? Why / why not?

7. Why does Winton have to focus on his writing after the accident? How important do you think this is in his career as a writer? Explain with specific reference to the text.

8. Do you think people prefer routine and 'predictability' in their lives?

9. How does 'havoc' play a crucial role in the human experience according to Winton?

10. Do you agree that 'havoc' is part of our lives and we know it is coming but not how it ends?

Human Experiences and 'Havoc: A Life in Accidents'

Winton's thesis is that havoc plays an integral role in the lives of people and he uses personal anecdotes to convey this and reveal something of himself and his family through the experiences that they have. While the anecdotes are personal the wider audience can see how these are applicable to every human experience, especially the trauma of the major incidents. Winton gives us the idea that from these experiences we will be changed and develop from them. He shows us the positives and negatives of these experiences and how they can include the general community and collective experiences.

We see collective experiences through the family, the police and the Christian congregation all of which are a type of 'family' in some definitions. The family are affected deeply by Winton's father's accident and his mother is subdued while being brave when in public. While his siblings are too young to fully appreciate the situation Winton is fully aware and he is a changed boy after the experience of having his father at home convalescing. The certainty that the family had is gone and their sense of safety lost. This is a traumatic experience for them all and it is a lengthy resolution.

Another collective experience can be seen in the concept of the police as family. They have their own set of rules and interactions as we see at the motorbike accident and the hospital. It is a difficult job and they have specific ways of coping with it. They are joined by their experiences and beliefs through seeing the worst in human nature and having distressing experiences on the job. We can also see this in the manner in which the Christian man integrates himself into the family and converts Winton's parents to Christianity. Religions have their own way of dealing with things and in this case we see his father's miraculous recuperation against the odds seen as 'an act of grace' and Winton has an 'open mind' about it all. We see her how attitudes change due to experiences and how human qualities, both good and bad, are brought out when havoc happens.

Winton also challenges the assumptions and beliefs of the reader by illustrating his story with extreme events to support his ideas that human experiences will happen we just don't know the outcome. He also states that these experiences show us who we are. Individuals respond in a variety of ways and we certainly get extreme reactions here; from the man who wants to fight rather than help his injured son to the woman Winton helps in her accident. While Winton's father is generally stoic we do see flashes of emotion;

> 'Sometimes there was no chat at all, just a hug that went on too long. On rare occasions there was muffled weeping behind closed doors.' (p37)

Winton also reveals how he is feeling about the experiences that he takes us on. These revelations create a sense of empathy as does the extreme emotions that the incidents he shares bring out. We see 'enraged', 'depression', 'anxieties' and 'fragile' all emotions that we can associate with. His experiences aren't exactly ours but they have commonalities that make his ideas come to fruition as we think about them. He also uses plenty of Australian terminology and colloquialisms to engage us and make the experience seem closer. He says without 'strife the copper and the novelist have nothing to work with.' He asks are we shaped by accidents?

'Betsy'

Les Winton was the only grandparent to drive a car and it was usually the ''35 flatbed Chev' but he also had a Harley. Our author could not understand why he 'purchased the dour little sedan he called Betsy'. It was a 1954 Hillman Minx an 'aesthetic travesty and an offence to youth'.

Winton clearly and cleverly describes everything he hates about the car and in hindsight he can 'smile at the memory' but at the time he felt 'shame' and never wanted to be seen in the car, especially as his grandfather's driving was 'nonconformist'.

Hillman Minx 1954 model by Charles01 - Own work, CC BY-SA 3.0,
https://commons.wikimedia.org/w/index.php?curid=7694692

Winton recalls how he could get a 'spasm of interest in oldish things' but didn't want to be defined by them. Other relatives had cars of 'style', even the 'sociopath' neighbour has cool car making him admit some old cars could be 'cool' but not the Hillman. This car wasn't even 'eccentric' like his grandmother, it stained the families 'honour'.

Eventually the car is passed to Winton's father who drives him to high school in it much to Winton's shame. He does 'everything in my power' to deny the car's existence and he feels it would do his reputation 'permanent damage'. Antipathy to the Hillman was the only thing that united the Winton siblings and they mounted a campaign to get rid of it. Their father refuses as he had an 'affection' for the car and knew it annoyed them.

Betsy is finally gone due to a major event. On a long trip they stop and eat Chinese and the father's 'irritable bowel' goes into overdrive. After an unscheduled pitstop he brings something back into the car along with the flies. In an amusing couple of paragraphs Winton describes the 'stench' and how the trip was a 'test of character for all'.

After this Betsy just seems to fade away and was replaced by an Austin Lancer which was 'daggy' but not socially catastrophic'. He then says Betsy represented the Menzian era and was enduring. He thinks he might have been a little harsh on the car but on second thoughts would still set fire to her.

Questions for 'Betsy'

1. Using the picture in the notes describe the Hillman Minx in your own words.

2. What kind of man was Les Winton?

3. Why do you think that Winton hates the car so much? Use specific quotes from the text to support your ideas.

4. What kind of teenager was Winton from the information that we get in the story?

5. Analyse why the father keeps the car despite the wishes of his children.

6. Discuss what Winton's mates think about the car. Do you think he worries too much about what others might think?

7. What leads to the demise of Betsy? Explain with specific reference to the text.

8. Give an example of irony in the story and state what it shows about Winton's personality and writing style?

9. Discuss the use of humour in the story focusing on ONE specific incident and what this reveals about human experience?

10. Here the human experience is told from an adult perspective but also through the eyes and experience of a teenager. How does this influence the thoughts of the reader?

Human Experiences and 'Betsy'

Betsy is an anathema to Winton because the car isn't what he sees as 'cool' from the perspective of a boy going into high school. It represents what is staid and in the past and it carries with it many assumptions. Winton is clearly motivated to rid his family of the car but is resisted by his father who knows that it annoys the children and he gets some pleasure from this fact. The car is a contradiction for the grandfather who rode a Harley motorbike and had a more eclectic lifestyle than the car would suggest. This is the paradox of human behaviour, perhaps people are not as predictable as we would like.

The viewpoint here is tinged with irony at times because Winton is looking back, reflecting on his more youthful self. We also see the humour in human experiences, his final comments about the car and his thought that we are 'merciless judges in our youth' still isn't enough to change his mind about burning the car. In some ways he is self-mocking in his irony about the obsolescence of the vehicle and in his dramatic descriptions of its faults. The humour that he derives from his father's painful experience in the long drive after the Chinese food still recognises the reality of the situation and the 'test of character' for the whole family seems amusing with the experience of time and age.

Winton makes much out of the experiences he had with the car and it made an impression with him that has lasted. He reflects personally on the experiences and judges the car harshly even with the passing of time. He is gently mocking of his father and grandfather without being cruel or disrespectful. Cars are central to many of our experiences and this the link that Winton makes.

Twice on Sundays

I

Two seemingly dichotomous quotes begin this story as Winton tells us of his Sundays which were exhausting because they were filled with religion. Sunday nights were the worst as after a day of worship they still had gospel service and 'Fellowship Tea'. Winton's family were 'evangelical fundamentalists' and very 'churchy'.

Sundays begin by picking up the local kids, whose parents are grateful they'd gone, and taking them to the church. Of course they would prefer to be at Scarborough Beach. Sunday school begins with singing but the scripture stories capture Winton's attention. He prefers the 'Jesus stuff' above all as the 'Nazarene was the hero of all boyhood heroes'. He tells of how the Wesleyan singing was loud and enthusiastic and how it united them as a 'team' for Jesus. After this the kids are returned to their parents and the non-driving pensioners get a lift for the eleven o'clock service. It is in the time between services where Winton meets his future wife, courting her by throwing stones!

Back in for the service it begins with a gentle, calming hymn. It was needed as the service is long before the climactic sermon which was always 'quite a show' in the tradition of their church. Winton says some were 'inspirational', 'haunting' and 'lyrical'. They head home for lunch and then it's on to family visitation. This includes his mother's parents who thought they were 'Jesus-creepers, fucking idiots' who had no fun. When this was over they headed home for the Sunday dinner.

The evening session was aimed at the 'younger crowd' and it was 'upbeat'. Compared to this day of church school was easy.

II

The church was 'my first and most formative culture', the opposite of Australian society at the time writes Winton. It was about *'What then must we do?'* as a philosophy and it was 'a childhood inoculation against social conformity'. The type of Christianity Winton was raised in was 'liberating and civilising' and they were 'doers'. The church had innumerable activities of all types and it gave the area 'a sense of coherence and communal spirit unmatched elsewhere.'

Winton also here discusses the literature of Patrick White who railed against 'prickly, philistine defensiveness' and an 'unreflective outlook'. This was not what Winton had in his church whose members had 'their sights set higher'.

III

Winton's parents were converts to a revivalist Church of Christ. Alexander Campbell, a founding father of the church said the Bible was 'a book of facts' but the more recent followers had mellowed somewhat yet the Bible was still the 'Word of God'.

The church was about authenticity and personal feelings which made prayer time interesting with its constant improvisation. There was no ritual, no ornamentation and the minister's tenure was subject to the congregation. The church was not subject to any outside authority and baptism was held back until you were of a responsible age. It was full immersion and Winton goes under at twelve. Baptism was more important than a wedding. The church itself was simple with only one wooden cross, yet the church service wasn't solemn and had 'lusty singing'.

IV

It was religion for 'humble folk' and the congregation were only working class who dressed up for Sundays. They were of 'modest education' but people who wanted to 'improve themselves'. Winton cites the case of Jeanette Winterson who wrote an expose of her own dealings with a sect 'far more severe and lurid' than Winton's but even she could see they had a 'thoughtful' life. The church gave them a place to think.

For Winton the church teaches him the 'beauty and power of language'. Bible study taught him the potency of language. They have discussions over specific words and how you read the right phrase or things can be 'catastrophic'. Some nights were 'tedious' but none were 'wasted' as he learns the use of metaphor. He caught the search for the 'right word' at church.

Yet in church and school you were still a 'captive', but at least you weren't invisible at church. You were noticed and even when you mucked about the older parishioners were 'patient'. When he became a teenager he was taken aside to be straightened out. It was harder to disappoint here than at school. The older folk took an interest in his 'walk' or spiritual life.

Once he asked a man, George Smith, about the size of his soul and Smith answers in a manner that 'rang true'. Winton is impressed and continues to be until today. He wonders if he could measure up to such a question and have the 'grace' that Smith had.

V

Winton's life was fully immersed in the church. They had everything but it was an 'enclave' of mutuality whose limitations couldn't go on forever. The 70s became a challenge as the world changed dramatically and their religion was 'static' and 'insufficient'. The mindset 'shrank and hardened' but the church wasn't safe from change. It became 'insular' and the group began to shows signs of stress.

Winton began to question as he got older and had 'new enthusiasms'. His ideas are unacceptable. Some other teens openly rebelled and left but some continued to pay lip-service to the church. Winton says he is a 'natural believer' and didn't need the parish to sustain his faith. Sometimes his defiance leaves his membership close to being ended as he disliked the 'right thinking and self-censorship'. It is of particular importance to him and he details arguments on 114–115.

He is initially 'humoured' by the elders and then they refuse to participate in discussion with him. He was never formally shunned he just 'slunk away'. For years Winton is perplexed by their behaviour but he realises they didn't have his education or language and he had 'shamed' them.

Winton then attends a more 'progressive' church but cannot put into language the ideas of grace and God. He still hears from members of his old church. Winton finds his best friends are 'refugees from evangelical fundamentalism' as they have some commonality from their experience. Winton now likes the liturgy and repetition of worship.

He misses some of the things from his religious youth, especially the singing. He is still a 'practising Christian' but can't determine which sort as he no longer thinks the 'rhetorical detail' important. He obviously still thinks about it and on Sunday evenings he still gets that 'old melancholy' he had in his youth.

Questions for 'Twice on Sundays'

1. After reading 'Twice on Sundays' discuss the relevance of the two quotes that begin the story.

2. Describe a typical Sunday in the Winton household.

3. Why was evening service more attractive to Winton, especially as he got older?

4. Why does Winton include specific examples from Patrick White and Jeanette Winterson? What effect do these examples have?

5. Analyse what type of people attended the church and how Winton perceives them.

6. Discuss what Winton's gained in terms of writing from his experiences in the church.

7. What experiences make Winton drift away from the church?

8. Describe the vignette about George Smith. Why is it included?

9. Discuss how Winton sees his current Christianity.

10. In this story the human experience is about the religious experiences he had growing up. How does this influence Winton's life?

Human Experiences and 'Twice on Sundays'

'Twice on Sundays' explores the human experience through the eyes of a religious upbringing and is a balanced examination of the process that Winton underwent. The overall impression that you get from reading the piece is that the experiences he has were genuinely positive and some of the later negative experiences were partly of his own making. It is interesting to note that he still writes that he is a 'practising Christian' which goes to the positivity of his faith and religious experiences.

His Church of Christ is a collective experience in that they are 'immersed' in the culture of the church which seems to provide all the experiences and makes the community what it is. This experience wanes as Winton becomes older and he feels confined by it but never seems to lose the faith that he has in God. He does lose faith in the Church itself and the narrow way it had of seeing the world. He notes that the world changes and the congregation became more insular in its thinking and outlook. I think he feels that it began to ignore the world and tried to become self-sufficient. You will be able to find many collective experiences that Winton had in the church to support your ideas.

Another set of human experiences that he discusses in the piece is that of the collective experiences of the family. Here we see how they all spend their Sundays from an early age. We read about the assumptions that they make about the world and the conflicting opinions of their wider family. Sundays are a long and arduous day for them all and it is a shared experience.

On an individual basis it is a very specific learning experience for Winton as he learns to see the inconsistencies in the churches view of the world. His time with the church teaches him faith and writing, he is a 'natural believer' but what he learns there about scripture teaches him the religion but also the power of language and its uses. It isn't wasted time but a time where he learns the reflective nature that is also essential to the writing experience.

We can also examine here the collective experience of the churchgoers and how their faith and joined experiences bind them together in a community of believers that stand together. The church makes the experience very personal as well and they share these experiences together. Winton also shows the other side when an individual leaves the community and gives examples of that as well.

'Twice on Sundays' is a thoughtful analysis of the human experiences in a community of evangelical fundamentalists without being critical or brutal of the people or the religion. Winton, perhaps because of the family connection, is very self-reflective in his discussion of his leaving and the people he encountered are viewed positively.

The Wait and the Flow

Winton begins by focussing on the point of surfing. It is something he had done most of his life and quickly he concludes 'there *is* no point'. It is addictive and mostly about waiting.

Winton grew up 'near Scarborough Beach' and the culture was surfing. He loved it from the age of five and after his first attempt he wanted to be a surfer.

He begins by riding a 'Coolite' made of Styrofoam which he later adapted for surfing. It causes a rash and he falls off a lot. Winton surfed for hours during the primary school years and in 1973 gets a proper surfboard which was a longboard 'relic'. He loved the 'sheer momentum' and the thrill he gets has never faded.

Surfing began in Polynesia where it was a symbol of power but also fun and was quickly adopted by the rest of the world. In Australia it had become an integral part of our culture and during the 50s it represented rebellion. It was an 'alternative to orthodoxy' where the natural world ruled.

Winton writes about the Romantic era of the 60s and early 70s. Surfing then had a special language of its own and they wanted *'flow'*. Then in the 80s it became a corporate activity and surfing became 'urban, aggressive, localised, greedy, racist and misogynistic'. At this point he gives it up and goes snorkelling.

Winton misses surfing and comes back to it when he finds a beach where the surfers are mellow. The 90s drags a lot of old surfers back when things on the water have changed. People begin to have fun again and more importantly women were getting back into the water. Winton sees surfing as 'meditative' and has no material result but rather a 'calibration of mood'.

Winton writes surfing helped him through the teenage years as it gave him 'respite' as it does now in his middle-age. He compares surfing to writing which is also about waiting. When something happens in both the 'feeling is divine'. Both have 'flow' when the energy arrives.

Questions for 'The Wait and the Flow'

1. From his initial observations how does Winton see the surfing experience?

2. How does the author become involved in surfing?

3. Discuss why Winton includes the information about the Polynesian origins of surfing.

4. How does Winton see surfing in the 1980s? Do some research and analyse if his analysis is accurate about the change in the sport.

5. Analyse what type of people attended the church and how Winton perceives them.

6. Discuss why Winton prefers the more 'mellow' aspects of surfing.

7. What experiences make Winton think that surfing results in a 'calibration of mood'?

8. Describe the comparison of surfing and writing. What are the similarities? Why is this important as an experiential thing for Winton?

9. Discuss why 'The Wait and the Flow' is a good title for this story.

10. In this story the human experience is about the surfing experience he enjoys so much. How does surfing influence Winton's life experiences?

Human Experiences and 'The Wait and the Flow'

In 'The Wait and the Flow' Winton describes the surfing experience and how it applies to other aspects of his life. Surfing is a communal sport in some ways and very individualistic in others. Winton points out how it adapted through the decades as a sport and how the different aspects of social change impinged on it. He is a very mellow surfer, uncompetitive and appreciative of nature. He freely admits there is no point to surfing and sees it as a meditation zone rather than having a materialistic value. He clearly states that it gives him respite and he can get in the 'flow'.

It is thought-provoking to note here that Winton experiences of surfing as a child and into his teens do not differ significantly from those he has when he re-enters the water as an adult. This shows that some experiences are significant and able to be reproduced. The idea that writing and surfing can produce a state of 'flow' is part of this and the 'waiting' that occurs in both is part of the 'divine' experience when the energy of creativity flows.

We also read that the surfing experience can be negative and significantly so as Winton leaves surfing for a time as the people surfing have brought the corporate values and materialistic practices into the water. The experience is tainted and far away from the initial values of surfing and man's interaction with the natural world. This interaction with the natural world is part of the experience and you can't control nature, nature controls the experience. We have seen in earlier notes how the human experience and nature are integral and is shared across time and cultures.

'In the Shadow of the Hospital'

Winton cites a song about 'That Hospital' in which the singer hypothesises that the hospital will always be there waiting for him. Hospitals have generally positive connotations for most people and Winton suggests words such as 'refuge', 'deliverance' and 'sanctuary'. He gives us the example of his son's injury in Greece and the race to the hospital. He writes *'In extremis'* we want a hospital desperately but at all other times the word brings 'dread' and he admits he has a phobia with hospitals although he'd rather call it an 'aversion'.

His earliest memories are of babies and adults spoke of it as a place where things get fixed. At the age of five he knows the hospital is 'trouble'. His earliest example is his father's accident which we read about earlier in these stories. Firstly his father takes an eternity to get back home and secondly when he does eventually get home he isn't in good shape. From then on his father is medicated, has innumerable visits to the doctors and then recovers. When his father returns to the hospital for further surgery Winton feels a 'chill of panic' so eventually his mother takes him to see this 'netherworld'.

It was a confronting environment for a child and visits were discouraged. He gets a 'weird tunnel vision' that he still has to this day which excludes the 'horrors, real and imagined'. His dad lifts him up and shows him the tubes and scars and Winton never wanted to go back. Winton then discusses a film, *Johnny Got His Gun*, about a quadruple amputee. It was a 'personal memory and nightmare' and he still sees it when he visits a hospital. Winton has spent a fair amount of time at hospitals for family reasons but has managed to avoid admission himself. Hospitals are part of family life but not specifically his life until the car accident he has at eighteen. He awakens in a hospital bed, 'stuck', and is so upset he begins to cry. He gets orange juice which he vomits up and just wants to 'flee'.

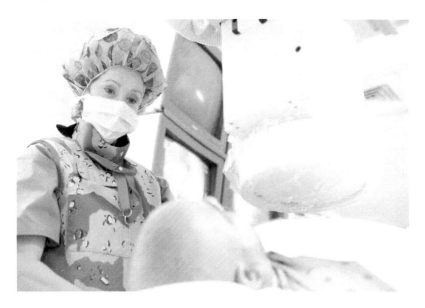

As an inpatient severe illness takes up all your brainpower which is a 'buffer'. Nobody tells you about the 'challenge of recovery'. Unless you're on heavy medication you can't sleep as it is so noisy. You become 'exhausted and 'agitated'. Your personality changes in that 'enclosed' world.

Great novels have been written set in hospitals and Winton gives examples which support that thesis. They make great settings because they have 'surreal logic'. He sees why terminal patients want to die at home.

Winton married a nurse and she brings her work home which is all the hospital he needs. Occasionally he visited her for lunch but was terrible company. He drove their baby there when she returned to work so it could be breastfed which he found 'odd' as people were dying upstairs.

Winton recalls how they lived in the shadow of Fremantle Hospital for five years. They had moved from a rural community and with three young children it seemed reassuring. Instead it provided twenty-four hour entertainment as all sorts of people came and went. The hospital had outgrown its space and began to spread which makes Winton claustrophobic. The hospital had its own 'microclimate' and it could change from a 'circus to a battlefield' and the residents needed to be aware of what was happening around them.

Hospitals are where people are open about their own narratives and emotions are strong. Their troubles are exposed and A&E is like a 'bright-lit hell'. Winton avoids it as he sees many bizarre things including mental health problems. It brings out the worst in people and you feel 'disgust' instead of sympathy. He admits kindness is still displayed especially by the 'nurses and paramedics'. Winton rarely enters the place but it grows 'oppressive' on him.

One day an estranged friend contacts him and asks Winton to visit him in the hospital as he has something to say. He goes to see the man and knows immediately he is close to death. They make their peace. Winton then comments on the birth of his first grandchild where his phobia again comes to the fore and he has to get out. They bring the child to him. Even nowadays he still has to gird himself for a visit. Winton's father is only alive because, 'They can do amazing things these days'.

Questions for 'In the Shadow of the Hospital

1.   What effect does the introduction about the song have on the audience?

2.   How, according to Winton, do people see hospitals 'In extremis'?

3.   Describe the effect of hospitals on Winton.

4.   Why does Winton come to the conclusion that hospitals are 'trouble' at an early age?

5.   Analyse Winton's own experience in hospital after the accident.

6.   Discuss the impact *Johnny Got His Gun* had on Winton.

7.   What experiences make Winton wary and weary about living near the hospital?

8.   Describe the cycle of the idea 'they can do amazing things these days'

9.   Discuss what shadow the hospital casts in the story. Think both literally and metaphorically in your response.

10.   In this story the human experience is about the hospital experience which is common to us all. How does living near Fremantle Hospital exacerbate Winton's experiences?

Human Experiences and 'In the Shadow of the Hospital'

In this piece on hospitals Winton covers substantial ideas on how hospitals impact on people and himself. Hospitals are an anathema to Winton and he doesn't engage with them unless completely necessary despite being married to a nurse and living opposite one for five years. He is to the point of phobia about them and nothing changes his position or assumptions from the age of five. It is worth noting that these ideas were based not on a personal experience but that of his father.

Hospitals encapsulate the entire spectrum of human emotions and Winton touches on many of them here. He states how they expose their narratives and emotions depending on their situation and the emergency section is the worst. The hospital has its own 'microclimate' which exacerbates these people's issues and there are few calming voices amidst the frenzy of activity. While Winton focuses on his perceptions and feelings in the hospital situation, these can be applied to the many that enter the hospital's environs.

It is interesting to note Winton develops a 'disgust' for these people's antics and the feel of the place becomes oppressive. Many of the assumptions he had when moving in from a rural setting have been evaporated and a more realistic/cynical attitude has developed as a result of his experiences. Winton never overcomes his phobia about the hospital and his experiences, even the birth of a grandchild, doesn't change him. They might be able to do amazing things but it doesn't alter the negatives he feels. It is an emotional rather than intellectual response.

The Demon Shark

I

Holy and Silent: On Peter Matthiessen's *Blue Meridian*

Australians have a cultural heritage of 'space' and the beaches of Winton's youth are an example of this. Here he is familiar with the sea and he loves to be near it. As a child he feels the ocean is 'utterly benign' and has no worries about it. As he gets older he discovers that it isn't as safe as he'd thought.

A trip to the movies and a short film called *'Savage Shadows'* changes things immediately. It showed a shark attack where Henri Bource lost a leg. The re-enactment looked so real that all of a sudden the water 'was never quite the same'. Peter Matthiessen writes about the 'shadow of sharks' and after that moment they were a presence in his mind when in the water.

Winton explains the fascination with beachside aquariums. In those days they were just tanks but even then people wanted to see the sharks which were 'appalling' and 'seductive'. Winton begins to study sharks in books and looked at pictures of shark attack pictures. Newspapers were full of shark attacks, warnings and lurid detail. Winton never got to see *Blue Water, White Death* which had the first footage of the great white shark but he did get to read Matthiessen's *Blue Meridian*, a book about the making of the movie.

Matthiessen is a superb writer of natural history and also fiction. In 1969 he joined Peter Gimbel, an American millionaire, to find and film the great white shark underwater. With the seven

Americans were Ron and Valerie Taylor, Australian shark experts, and Ron was the 'best diver alive' at the time. They head to Durban and in a feeding frenzy of dead whale two Americans leave the cage and Valerie is trapped inside when a shark enters the open gate but she survives.

GREAT WHITE SHARK

Gimbel's reckless behaviour divides the crew and Matthiessen begins to concentrate his story on the Taylor's, especially Ron, with whom he seems fascinated. As the ship heads around the Indian Ocean in search of sharks; the differences in culture between the crew members shows. Gimbel takes bigger risks and Matthiessen and the Taylor's think it reckless while Gimbel had a 'sense of immunity'.

Finally the group moves to the Spencer Gulf in South Australia where they are joined by Rodney Fox, a 360 stitch veteran of a great white attack. Here they find the shark they are looking for and it's 'awesome' so they get into the water and begin filming excitedly. Matthiessen is 'horrified' at the sharks as they show an 'implacable need' to feed. Even he reaches out to touch as the shark goes past.

Gimbel's mission was over and Matthiessen thinks Gimbel was searching for something in himself. Winton writes that Matthiessen's curiosity with nature is still alive and the Taylor's now see sharks differently since that time in 1969. Winton also knows that sharks still take people and while this is true he still envies the touch Matthiessen had of 'the living shadow'.

II

Predator or Prey?

Australians have a demon that 'is silent and it swims'. The media blows up stories about sharks to make money and entice viewers and most Australians have 'an irrational fear and disgust for the shark' and Winton admits to this as a youth but he never saw a live one. He did see dead ones as people hunted them and hung them as trophies. Winton notes the sad waste and thinks people had 'declared war on them'. He sees them shot in Albany as a thirteen year old near the whaling station and it doesn't bother him at the time.

Now he's different and the 'culture has changed' for all animals except the shark which he claims 'nobody cares' about. Winton begins to make a case for the shark's preservation as it emerged in prehistory and is vital ecologically but we see it as a killer which gives 'humankind the licence to do the unspeakable'. He comments on the 'barbaric' shark fin trade which is helping the decline of the shark worldwide.

Winton decries the slaughter and states they are not 'evil' and sharks deserve to be understood. His personal experience of some has been positive. He applauds the idea that most people have moved on from the 'ignorant prejudices' of the past although some who have no idea like 'politicians and shock jocks' still moan about sharks and stir up hysteria. In 2011 four people were killed by sharks and people were scared to go into the water but nearly 1300 were killed in car accidents and people kept driving.

Sharks should be afraid of people we kill so many every day and more decline is 'potentially catastrophic' for the ocean's ecology. Winton argues we need to change and 'reform our attitude' before it is too late for the sharks and us.

III

Passing Strangers

Winton here gives us a personal anecdote that binds together this piece on sharks. He sees the weather is perfect for surfing, jumps in his ute and heads down to the beach. On the beach a disintegrating whale carcass interests his dog and he notices it doesn't smell as bad as it did a month or two ago. Out on the break with a few locals he learns the three 'bronzies' are still about. He surfs for a while and then he is bumped by one of the three sharks which then flees. He is filled with 'awe and terror'.

Winton tells another surfer who heads to the beach immediately. Winton continues to surf and then he catches a wave that takes him directly at another of the bronze whalers which 'bolts' at the last second. Winton keeps surfing he is so 'buzzed' but eventually goes in.

As a footnote Winton tells us of a pointless government shark cull which was later modified after public outcry. Significantly an infinitesimal number of people die from shark attacks compared to road accidents or cancer.

Questions for 'The Demon Shark'

1. How does Winton convey the concept of 'space' and his love of the beach?

2. Describe the effect *Savage Shadows* has on Winton.

3. How does Matthiessen describe sharks?

4. Winton states people are fascinated with sharks. How does he explain this fascination?

5. Analyse Winton's thoughts on *Blue Meridian*.

6. Discuss how the crew on Gimbel's ship become divided over safety.

7. What experience does Matthiessen have that Winton is jealous of?

8. Discuss the argument(s) Winton makes for saving the sharks. Analyse how he uses personal experience to convey his ideas.

9. Analyse the use of the footnote to conclude. How does this enhance (or detract) from the argument/effect Winton is making?

10. In this story the human experience is about the environment and the human need for nature which is bigger than just one individual's experiences. How does Winton convey the concept of the need to preserve the shark in terms of human experiences past and present?

Human Experiences and 'The Demon Shark'

In 'The Demon Shark' Winton points out that prejudices and assumptions about something, in this instance sharks, are damaging. He also shows us that attitudes can change over time by how things are perceived by collective groups. The main aspect, in my opinion, that is expressed here is that human experiences are inescapably linked to the natural world and that our behaviours can disrupt this causing issues and 'catastrophic' consequences.

Winton highlights the negative attitude toward sharks, mainly through misunderstandings, has created an atmosphere where people are terrified and vengeful. He is attempting, through illustrating other human experiences, how this isn't true and that sharks, especially the white pointer, are primal creatures who are instinctive, not vindictive or 'evil'.

Winton analyses the assumptions that have been made about the shark and the cruelties they have endured because of these assumptions. He notes changing social attitudes but paradoxically the shark seems to be defined in a category on its own. Winton attempts to change the attitudes of the reader through his own readings and personal experiences – realistic interactions that bring positive outcomes. He notes the contradictions in human attitudes and the inane comments of those with little or no experience(s) to draw upon.

Winton also highlights the impact of nature on human experiences and how the two are eternally linked; 'their survival is bound up in our own'. This is a significant facet as with a distorted environment we are susceptible to damaging our own experiences.

Barefoot in the Temple of Art

Winton in this story discusses his return visit to the National Gallery of Victoria or 'The Kremlin of St Kilda Road'. His first visit as a child was tinged with embarrassment as his family are initially denied entry as they have bare feet. The family have a type of isolation complex coming from Western Australia and this is a weeklong car ride to Melbourne to sample the 'Other Side'.

Initially Melbourne is a bit underwhelming because of their expectations but the gallery had a water feature which was a blessing in the heat. Adults told them to get out as it was being 'disrespectful' to the art. After being initially being refused entrance their father talked his way in by saying they were Queenslanders. Winton actually hides behind Moore's *Draped Seated Woman* until he regains his composure. He is then able to take the place in with French's 'much discussed stained-glass ceiling' first followed by Australian art, European art (such as Rembrandt pictured) and the modern art which at the time he 'didn't understand'. It was a huge building and he is 'giddy' moving around until he has to leave. It fired his imagination to be a writer.

Now entering the gallery again he immediately sees changes in name and structure and the building is 'teeming with visitors' and it is not so intimidating as it was. People now play in the water with immunity and children are welcome. He revisits the Moore statue and admires Conte's *Tree of Life*. He also rediscovers what he saw last visit but draws on the new art as well.

Winton also reflects on changing attitudes. The 'young and uninitiated' are no longer spurned. Asian art has emerged and

Winton particularly comments on Purnomo's Orang Hilang, a political piece from Indonesia. Winton spends a day wandering and only sees a 'fraction' of the art. He recollects his boyhood visit when he arrived barefoot but left 'like a man in boots'.

Questions for 'Barefoot in the Temple of Art'

1. Why are the Winton family in Melbourne?

2. Winton is embarrassed by his father. What does this anecdote show about the family?

3. Why is Winton drawn to the water at the gallery?

4. What impression does the experience of the gallery have on Winton?

5. How has the gallery changed over time? Why is Winton more positive about it?

6. Discuss how he shows us changing attitudes in Australia.

7. Discuss why Winton includes the last paragraph. What impression does it leave with the reader?

8. Is Winton positive or negative about his experiences at the gallery? Give evidence to support your ideas.

9. Analyse the use of the specific examples of art that he mentions. How does this draw us into his story?

10. In 'Barefoot in the Temple of Art' the human experience is about culture and the impact it can have on an individual and their experiences during and after. Does he make a convincing argument for the cultural experience?

Human Experiences and 'Barefoot in the Temple of Art'

The human experiences shown in 'Barefoot in the Temple of Art' focus on the changing attitude in Australia toward the arts and the wider world in general over the period of time between the two experiences Winton had in visiting the National Gallery of Victoria now the NGV International which says something in itself. Winton tells us about his experiences but this allows us to see the broader development in Australian interaction with the world so that our collective experiences are wide-ranging and less parochial.

Winton's first visit showed a more staid cultural experience, nearly elitist in its approach where art was unsuitable for the masses. He was not welcome to touch the water on the way in and children weren't all that welcome. This is the first thing we notice changes. On his next visit everyone has their hands in the water and children are welcome, even catered to. The name change also indicates a change in thinking of the collective Australian ethos that it is now 'International' and carries the assumptions that go with that as opposed to the 'White Australia policy' that precluded such thoughts.

We can also examine the concept of experience that Winton brings to his second visit. It is somewhat about the experience gathered over time but also the development of enrichment of cultural experiences and travel. Winton brings a different language to the experience and while the first enthralling visit changed his perspective he brings more judgement to the second.

THE ESSAY

The essay consists of the basic form of an introduction, body paragraphs and conclusion. The esssay has been the subject of numerous texts and you should have the basic form well in hand. As teachers, the point we would emphasise would be to link the paragraphs both to each other and back to your argument (which should directly respond to the question). Of course, ensure your argument is logical and sustained.

Make sure you use specific examples and that your quotes are accurate. To ensure that you respond to the question, make sure you plan carefully and are sure what relevant point each paragraph is making. It is solid technique to actually 'tie up' each point by explicitly coming back to the question.

When composing an essay the basic conventions of the form are:

- State your argument, outline the points to be addressed and perhaps have a brief definition.

A solid structure for each paragraph is:
- Topic sentence (*the main idea and its link to the previous paragraph/ argument*)
- Explanation/ discussion of the point including links between texts if applicable.
- Detailed evidence (*Close textual reference - quotes, incidents and technique discussion.*)
- Tie up by restating the point's relevance to argument/ question

- Summary of points
- Final sentence that restates your argument

As well as this basic structure, you will need to focus on:

Audience – for the essay the audience must be considered formal unless specifically stated otherwise. Therefore, your language must reflect the audience. This gives you the opportunity to use the jargon and vocabulary that you have learnt in English. For the audience ensure your introduction is clear and has impact. Avoid slang or colloquial language including contractions (like 'doesn't', 'e.g.', 'etc.').

Purpose – the purpose of the essay is to answer the question given. The examiner evaluates how well you can make an argument and understand the module's issues and its text(s). An essay is solidly structured so its composer can analyse ideas. This is where you earn marks. It does not retell the story or state the obvious.

Communication – Take a few minutes to plan the essay. If you rush into your answer it is almost certain you will not make the most of the brief 40 minutes to show all you know about the question. More likely you will include irrelevant details that do not gain you marks but waste your precious time. Remember an essay is formal so **do not** do the following: story-tell, list and number points, misquote, use slang or colloquial language, be vague, use non-sentences or fail to address the question.

PLAN:

Don't even think about starting without one!

> *Introduce...*
>
> the texts you are using in the response
>
> *Argument*: The human experience is affected by:
> - Idea One
> - Idea Two
> - Idea Three

You need to let the marker know what texts you are discussing. You can start with a definition but it can come in the first paragraph of the body. You MUST state your argument in response to the question and the points you will cover as part of it. Wait until the end of the response to give it!

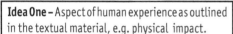

> **Idea One** – Aspect of human experience as outlined in the textual material, e.g. physical impact.
>
> **Idea Two** – Another aspect of human experience as outlined in the textual material, e.g. psychological impact.
> - explain the idea
> - where and how is it shown in the prescribed text?
> - where and how is it shown in related text 1?
>
> **Idea Three** – People's sense of experience is affected by context and environment
> - explain the idea
> - where and how shown in the prescribed text?
> - where and how shown in related text 1?

You can use the things you have learned to organise the essay. For each one, you say where you saw this in your prescribed text and where in related text(s).

Two or three ideas are usually enough as you can explore them in detail.

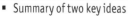

> - Summary of two key ideas
> - Final sentence that restates your argument

Make sure your conclusion restates your argument. It does not have to be too long.

MODEL ESSAY OUTLINE

> **To what extent are human experiences significant in the set text?**
>
> **From your studies respond to this question using your set text and at ONE piece of other textual material**

This essay needs to be attacked in a manner that responds to the question and shows ALL your knowledge about the text. The question lends itself to a close study of Tim Winton's *The Boy Behind the Curtain* as the text does show how the human experience is integral to life and how it shapes our other experiences and interaction with the world.

An introduction might be written:

> Human experiences are important in Winton's non-fiction *The Boy Behind the Curtain* and the two related texts Lawrence's film *Jindabyne* and Ed Sheeran's song *Castle on the Hill*. These texts show how human experiences are integral to human existence and bring more meaning to one's life. Life is about experiences that challenge us and define how we see the world. They shape our beliefs and attitudes and can be confronting at the same time. Without experiences our lives would be empty and meaningless.

Your essay should then follow the outlined plan and develop these ideas. This gives you the opportunity to link the texts and fully develop each of the ideas.

ANNOTATED RELATED MATERIAL: DIFFERENT STUDIES OF HUMAN EXPERIENCES

Jindabyne – **Ray Lawrence**

Jindabyne is an Australian film that captures a wide array of human experiences. It touches on the ideas mentioned in the introduction to this text in a number of detailed instances. We can begin by considering the following before beginning a detailed examination of the narrative.

The collective human experience:

- Aboriginality and the spiritual;
- The Fishermen and their code;
- The reaction of the townsfolk;
- Media response;
- Interaction with the natural world.

Individual Experience:

- An individual character's response to the body – choose one;
- The killer;
- Response to the revelations;
- Past experiences and how they impact on current experiences;
- Reaction to loss – emotional;
- Assumptions about life.

We can now look at the plot to help us understand each of these issues. *Jindabyne* begins with the sound of a radio being tuned and the Australian feel of the movie is immediate with the theme music for the ABC news. Lawrence emphasises the isolation by having the radio not tune in correctly for an unknown female character, forcing her to use the cassette player. With this unusual beginning we know that her experience is not going to be positive.

We then pan to the rocks slowly where Gregory, our killer, sits patiently in a truck with the engine running watching the road. We know he is prepared for this as he has binoculars. He sees an Aboriginal girl, Susan O'Connor, driving and she is the one fiddling with the radio. He chases her down and forces her to stop. He moves toward her as we see a long shot of how isolated they are. We see his face in her window looming above her and screaming about the electricity coming down from the mountains. This film is no murder mystery, as we know from the beginning that the murderer is Gregory the electrician. This is about the experiences of the other characters in the film and how they respond to current experiences.

The Kane family, Stewart, Claire and son Tom, is waking. Claire pretends to sleep, before waking suddenly and being affectionate with Tom. Stewart and Tom head out fishing. The scene doesn't feel quite right and there is some emotional tension between Stewart and Claire that is unspoken due to what they have experienced in the past. Claire had a complicated past when she was pregnant with Tom. When she finds she is pregnant again, she becomes emotional and slightly unstable.

As the film builds we see the complex pasts of the characters and their interactions in the confinement of the small town. The fishing trip is a break from this and extremely important in their lives.

We see some of the emotional instability in characters such as Caylin-Calandria, who with Tom, has some issues at school. Along with Caylin-Calandria, Claire and Jude also have issues but in a nicely framed shot of the three female characters, we see them conform as members of a close knit group. The sacrifice they make is similar to Gregory's but on a different scale. Note the connection here and how each one is to get back to order and societal norms. This is the collective experience for all the characters.

At the Kanes' home the tensions are obvious from their past experiences but they contain it for appearances' sake. Occasionally, the tension reaches breaking point and the experience strains the superficial approach. The tension builds at home and the fishing trip seems like a good opportunity to break the cycle.

When we see Gregory dump Susan O'Connor's body in the river, we know that the fishing and her death will interact.

The next morning, the fishermen head off for their one big trip of the year and the sign 'Gone fishing' is put in the garage window. We see Billy on the phone to Elissa and putting the sign the wrong way round in the window shows his immaturity. They have already said they are taking him away to make a man of him. The four men have a few beers on the way and talk as they travel through the landscape. They intend to give Billy the experience they think he needs as a 'man' — a cultural rite of passage.

The men arrive and the high-tension electricity wires punctuate the wilderness. They begin to hike toward the valley. It's a long walk in and the terrain is hilly and difficult. They stop on the way and again we see Billy's naivety when Stewart says 'Listen to that' meaning the silence but he can't, as he has his earphones in. It is part of the break in tension of the film that they commune with nature. This experiential break affects all the men. The episode represents a distinct human experience.

Stewart wanders down the river fishing and sees Susan's body caught in the rocks. Hesitantly, he wades out to it and turns it over saying 'Oh Jesus' repeatedly. He screams for the others to come as he drags the body to the bank. He is obviously upset, making the sign of the cross. Stewart tells Rocco to 'take her, for fuck's sake, take her' and their shock is obvious. They all stare at the body and Billy goes to run off but they stop him. The four men meet and decide to leave her in the water and tie her so she doesn't float away.

The presence of the body threatens to detract from the enjoyment of the fishing experience. The act of attempted isolation of the bad experience is expected to evoke only a mild response. They do not anticipate the stormy reaction it receives when they return to the community.

The men go on fishing, with Stewart getting the first big fish on an absolutely perfect day. The lure of the fish is strong, especially when they see the big one he has caught. They have a successful and enjoyable time, a positive experience. They get a photo of the catch and Billy holds up his fish in a typical hunter/gatherer pose. Capturing an experience this way is most enjoyable.

It is a photo that will come back to haunt them as things change back in the world. An unanticipated adverse reaction can be a horrific experience.

Stewart goes to check on the dead girl, rolling her over and getting debris off her face in a quite tender gesture. The next day they head back and report it. At the car Billy rings Elissa and says they found a body but 'caught the most amazing fish'. They are told by the police to wait and seem despondent their trip has been ruined. They organise their story as Stewart says they have 'to get their story straight'.

We cut to Gregory eating breakfast and he appears to be a normal, lonely man until he goes out to his shed where he has hidden Susan's car and this reminds us of the evil in him. Consider his experience and his motivations. How does he see his actions and the world?

The next day at the station the policeman tells the fishermen 'we don't step over bodies for our recreational pursuits' and 'the whole town's ashamed of you'. When they are told to 'piss off' from the station the press are waiting for them and Billy makes a comment. Carl is angry with the press but we can begin to see signs of distress within the whole group.

The experience they had so looked forward to has become a negative one and the tensions we saw before are exacerbated by the emotional and collective response to the murder. Claire soon becomes obsessed with the whole affair because of her own state. The newspaper the next day has the headline, 'Men fish over dead body' because Billy has talked. Billy is late to work and Stewart tells him they have to 'stick together on this'.

Susan's sister calls them 'animals' and raises the race question by asking if they would have left a white girl. The Aboriginal youths begin to attack and vandalise the property of the men in violent outbursts, including throwing a rock through Billy's van window and thus endangering his baby. They insult Carl at the caravan park and vandalise the garage.

The police aren't any help and the situation deteriorates. Jude tells the police they shouldn't be enforcing the 'political correctness' laws. The intervention of the sense of Aboriginality and race challenges the assumptions people have and how we see the world. The contrasting views are ingrained in the social structures and part of different collective experiences.

The Aboriginal people see the white people as 'interfering' and the group of fishermen begin to fight amongst themselves. Elissa says they shouldn't go to the bush at all as it's sacred. The group talk about the bush and Rocco punches Stewart for saying the Aborigines are superstitious. The experience of racial tension becomes ever-present and adds to the emotional responses to the experience.

We now head slowly to a resolution of the conflict brought about by the various experiences. Each is handled in a different manner by characters and you can explore one or two of the responses. To cycle back to the original murder, Claire is stalked by Gregory in his truck. He stops her but drives off after staring weirdly, an odd experience in itself.

Terry and Stewart talk and Stewart meets Rocco and Carl. He tells them Claire's left him 'again'. Rocco can't believe it and we cross cut to her looking out into the wilderness after he looks thoughtfully out the window. These different reactions to experiences mirror attitudes in life and reactions to emotional and intellectual conflict.

In conclusion, Lawrence takes us back to the healing power of nature in our human experiences when the Aboriginal people are having a ceremony. Gregory watches while Claire walks in. Again we see his truck as an omnipresent force in the film, almost an extension of him. An Aboriginal man tells Claire to 'piss off' from the ceremony after she says she has come to pay her 'respects' but he is told to leave her alone by an Auntie.

The smoke and tribal music symbolise the ceremonial nature of the setting and the camera pans around the scene and the bush. We see parts of the ceremony with chanting and clapping sticks. The camera moves in and out while other shots pan around the bush, giving us the full experience and Lawrence portrays this as a positive, healing experience.

Eventually Stewart, Tom, Carl, Jude and Rocco arrive to pay respects. Tom runs to his mother and Stewart goes over and says 'Sorry' but is rebuffed by the father who throws dirt on him and spits, refusing his apology. Then an Aboriginal girl tells a little about Susan's story and sings the last love song Susan wrote.

The camera pans around all the faces as they listen to the song and the ceremonial smoke wafts around. It seems to have some healing effect on everyone, as it is a meaningful experience which raises the idea of the spiritual experience in the text. The girl stops singing through emotion. 'Be gone' seems to symbolise in language the whole scenario for each character.

We see a long wide shot of the bush before fading back to Gregory waiting again in his car behind the rocks for another victim. It is quite a circular conclusion and it is an odd end when he crushes the fly. We don't quite know what to make of the whole experience and he seems to be the only character unchanged by the experiences in the film.

Poem: 'Inland' by John Kinsella

The poem captures the mood and ethos of the outback farming communities and deals with the human aspect more than some of the other poems in Kinsella's collection: *Peripheral Light*. This poem is one long restless thought that mimics memories and recollection while raising the current, topical issues that concern the poet. As usual with his poems Kinsella orientates the audience early with the word 'Inland' and then continues the poem without a full stop. The poem flows with the use of commas but Kinsella allows us to stop and think with the use of the colon, brackets and the hyphen. Look for these punctuation stops as you read as they emphasise a specific point or idea that resonates with the audience.

The first stanza gives us a foreshadowing of the events to follow with the warnings in the words 'storm', 'alert' and 'uncertain'. This ominous tone is reinforced by the word 'ghosts' and the implication of death which is constant in much of Kinsella's poetry. The next stanza deals with a more human element and we get the country feel with the bracketed gossip about McHenry's accident which shows the close knit community. Habits here are formed as part of survival and known to all as we see 'the old man plying the same track' and the families possibly heading to church on the Sunday morning.

The third stanza returns to the vagaries of nature. Kinsella repeats 'uncertain' with regard to the weather. Weather and the environment play a large role in farming communities and it is especially so at sowing and harvest. Despite the uncertainty and 'ashen' days which alter 'moods', the community returns to their habits and routines which shape their lives. The next stage returns to the road and the implication of a journey but a journey that is straight and in conflict with the cycles of the natural world. The path seems already marked and measured. It is 'straight and narrow', marked by a theodolite.

The final four lines of the poem are pure Kinsella, marking the transience of humanity on the landscape. We read

> 'it's a place of borrowed dreams
> where the marks of the spirit
> have been erased by dust –
> the restless topsoil'

The European farmers had 'borrowed dreams' for their own relationship with the land but this line also harks back to the indigenous Dreamtime when the land was created. The indigenous view that the land owns the people is also true for Kinsella. This sense of nobody owning the land is strong in his poetry. European impact on the land can be seen in the spirituality being removed by the dust—dust created by the poor farming techniques transferred from a different land. He finishes with the 'restless topsoil' as if the whole earth is moving in its own discontented journey, just as the people move.

The influence here of genuinely lost spirituality and connection with the land as we move directly on the 'high road' contrasts with the more flowing, 'restless' side of the natural world. This visual contrast is obvious but we can also discuss the contrast between habit and spirit. 'Inland' is a poem that uses the landscape to show the contrast between two views of the countryside.

DRAMA: Eugene O'Neil's *Desire Under the Elms*

O'Neill sets out to instruct how the house and elms should appear and the year is 1850. Note how he describes the 'enormous' elms as,

> 'exhausted women resting their sagging breasts and hands and hair on its roof, and when it rains their tears trickle down monotonously and rot on the shingles'

and how they dominate and 'rot'. It is important to read this both in terms of the play and in the context of American theatre. The description here shows O'Neill's genius at new design and original theatricality.

Part One: Scene One

The whole first page and a third are nearly all playwright notes that describe the farm, the house and the characters of Eben, Simeon and Peter. The first words of the play, 'God! Purty!' reflect the beauty of the land and how Eben perceives it. Eben is 'resentful and defensive' and feels 'trapped' on the farm.

His older half-brothers Simeon and Peter are 'more bounce and homelier in face, shrewder and more practical.' They all have worked hard on their father's farm over the years and have little feeling for their absent father. We learn that Simeon had a 'woman' who died and that Peter is excited by the prospect of 'gold in the West'. They all talk about how hard they've worked and hope that the father might 'die soon'. What we get from all this is that they are earthy and this is reflected in their bodies and clothes which are all dirt stained.

We also see here the difference between them as Eben sees gold in the pasture, not California, as they head in for a dinner of bacon in what seems a ritual they have performed many times before. Note that O'Neill calls for the use of the curtain at the end of the scene.

Scene Two

It is twilight and again we get detailed notes on the interior scene. Simeon tells Eben he should not wish their father dead and Eben replies he's not his son but, 'I'm Maw – every drop of blood!' He then blames the father, Ephraim Cabot, for killing his mother by working her to death but the others just say there was work to be done. O'Neill gets them to list the jobs and Eben comes back with 'vengeful passion' that, while they did nothing, he will see his mother gets 'rest and sleep in her grave!'

They then discuss Cabot's absence and how he just drove off in a buggy one day in a rush. Simeon says that when he went,

'He druv off in the buggy, all spick an' span, with the mare all breshed an' shiny, druv off clackin' his tongue an' wavin' his whip. I remember it quite well'

Eben mocks Simeon for not stopping him and the scene concludes with Eben leaving to see Minnie the town whore. We learn all the Cabot men have slept with her. Simeon and Peter say that Eben is just like 'Paw' and thinks of California. The final image is of Eben with his arms stretched to the sky talking about starts and sin, 'my sin's as purty as any one on 'em!', until he 'strides' to the village for Min.

Scene Three

It is 'pitch darkness' and Eben comes home with the news that Cabot has married a 'purty' thirty-five year old. He has heard this in the village and this effectively disinherits the boys. Simeon and Peter see California as their only option now. Eben tells the boys that they can have three hundred dollars each if they sign their share of the farm over to him. He can get the money as his mother told him,

> 'I know whar it's hid. I been waitin' – Maw told me. She knew whar it lay fur years, but she was waitin'....It's her'n – the money he hoarded from her farm an' hid from Maw. It's my money by rights now.'

They think about it and Eben tells them about his night with Min. He tells how he hates the new wife after the boys suggest he might sleep with her, just like Min, to get the old man back. Peter and Simeon say they'll do the deal and leave the farm. Both are bitter and vindictive about Cabot.

Scene Four

The setting is the same as Scene Two and the boys are discussing how they don't have to work now – it is all down to Eben who is jubilant as he thinks it will all be his. Peter and Simeon again reflect on how like his father he is, 'Like his Paw'. They also tell he isn't much of a milker but they soon talk about their leaving and how they'll miss some aspects of the farm.

Eben comes back in and says that the 'old mule an the bride' are coming. The two older boys begin to pack and sign Eben's papers as he gives them the money Cabot had hidden. They tell him they'll send him 'a lump o' gold for Christmas' and head into the yard feeling 'light' because of their newfound freedom.

Ephraim Cabot and Abbie Putnam then come in and O'Neill describes them in detail. Cabot is

> 'seventy-five, tall and gaunt, with great, wiry, concentrated power, but stoop shouldered by toil. His face is hard as if it were hewn from a boulder, yet there is a weakness in it'

but his face is weakened with petty pride. Abbie is

> 'thirty-five, buxom, full of vitality. Her round face is pretty but marred by its rather gross sensuality. There is strength and obstinacy in her jaw, a hard determination in her eyes, and about her whole personality.'

She also has a 'desperate quality'. Cabot shows Abbie the place and she says to him it's 'mine'. Then he sees the two boys not working. He introduces Abbie and she goes to look at 'her' house and they warn her Eben's inside.

Cabot tells them to get to work and they give him cheek, saying they are 'free' and heading to California. They 'whoop' it up and he says he'll have them chained up. They throw rocks at the house, smashing the window and head off singing. Abbie sticks her head out the window and says she likes the room but he is thinking of the stock and 'almost runs' to the barn.

Abbie then meets Eben in the kitchen and talks to him in 'seductive tones'. She says she doesn't want to be his 'Maw' but friends and he cusses her. She tells him of her troubled life and how Cabot gave her a chance to escape it. He calls her a 'harlot' and they argue over ownership of the farm. She has the upper hand in law and he leaves but the seeds of their growing attraction have been set.

Outside he and his father argue about life and work and he tells Eben 'Ye'll never be more'n half a man!' The scene ends with Abbie washing up and the faint notes of the song the boys were singing as they left.

Part Two: Scene One

Again O'Neill describes in detail the farmhouse setting. Two months have passed and it is a hot Sunday afternoon. Abbie in her best outfit is sitting on the porch and Eben comes out of the house also dressed in his best. They stalk each other, both attracted and repelled. As he walks away she 'gives a sneering, taunting chuckle' at him and they argue but the attraction is obvious. She says that nature will pull him to her but he says that she is married and he goes to leave her.

She accuses him of going to Min and she gets angry stating he'll never get the farm,

> 'Ye'll never live t' see the day when even a stinkin' weed on
> it 'll belong t' ye!'

He says he hates her and leaves as Cabot enters. She tells him Eben has been mocking him and twists the conversation to the inheritance of the farm. She tells him Eben lusts after her and as he angers she backs off in her accusations. Reassured, he says that she can have the farm if she bears the son she says she wants with him. He says that he'd 'do anythin' ye axed, I tell ye!' if she gave him a son and tells her to pray to God for it to happen.

Scene Two

It is about eight in the evening and here the bedrooms are highlighted, with Eben in one and Cabot with Abbie in the other. The two of them are talking about a son. They seem together, yet apart, as he tells her of his life on the farm and how God's hard. He both lost and gained on the way through, but the farm is his. He says he is pleased he found her, his 'Rose o' Sharon'. Abbie promises him that she will bear a son as he basically threatens her,

> 'Ye don't know nothin' – nor never will. If ye don't hev a son t' redeem ye...'

and he leaves to sleep in the barn with the cows 'whar it's restful'.

We then see Eben and Abbie restless and she leaves the room and goes to him. He 'submits' to her kisses then 'hurls' her away. Abbie says she'd make him 'happy' and she knows he wants her too much. She tells him to go down to the parlour and he is shocked as this is where his mother was 'laid out'. She leaves for the parlour and he wonders what's happening. The scene closes with a question to his dead mother, 'Maw! Whar are yew?' but we know that he wants her and will go to her.

Scene Three

The scene now shifts to the parlour which is described as a 'grim, repressed room like a tomb'. Abbie waits and Eben appears and he sits at her invitation. They talk about his Maw and how they hate Cabot. Abbie throws herself at him with 'wild passion' and he is caught up in the moment and thinks that it's his Maw wanting him to sleep with Abbie to get revenge on Cabot,

I see it! I sees why. It's her vengeance on him – so's she
kin rest quiet in her grave!

Abbie proclaims her love for him and he for her then they kiss 'in
a fierce, bruising kiss' to close the scene.

Scene Four

A more bold and confident Eben leaves the house and Abbie opens
the parlour window. She calls him over for a kiss and they talk a
bit before Eben says his Maw can now rest. They split as Cabot
comes out of the barn but are now obviously in love. Eben tells
Cabot that his Maw is now at rest and Cabot says he rests best
with the cows. Cabot is confused but the scene ends with him
criticising Eben as 'Soft-headed' and a 'born fool' but, being a
practical man, he heads for breakfast.

Part Three: Scene One

Time has passed to 'late spring the following year'. Eben is upstairs
in emotional and psychological conflict while a party happens
downstairs. Cabot has drunk too much and Abbie sits, pale and
thin, in a rocking chair. There is a fiddler and Abbie begins the
scene by asking for Eben and the guests 'titter' as most think the
baby is Eben's, not Cabot's, which is true enough. They laugh and
Cabot is angered by this and orders them to dance. The fiddler
'slyly' says they're waiting for Eben but Cabot mocks the boy and
then ensues a bawdy conversation about his fertility,

I got a lot in me – a hell of a lot – folks don't know on.
Fiddle 'er up, durn ye! Give 'em somethin' t' dance t!'

The fiddler plays and they dance. Cabot joins in frantically and 'whoop(s)' it up. He exhausts the fiddler and pours whiskey. In the upstairs room Eben is looking at the baby. Abbie goes upstairs and Cabot leaves for outside, 'fresh air', as she has told him not to 'tech' her. The guests gossip after he goes and we see Eben and Abbie upstairs and she professes her love for him,

> 'Don't git feelin' low. I love ye, Eben. Kiss me.'

Cabot says he's going to rest in the barn. The scene concludes with the fiddler playing in celebration of 'the old skunk gittin' fooled!'

Scene Two

Eben is outside half an hour later and Cabot is coming back from the barn. Cabot tells him to get a woman inside and he might get a farm. Eben replies that this farm's his and Cabot mocks him. He tells her Abbie has been promised the farm for her son and Eben is angered thinking Abbie has tricked him.

Eben goes to kill her but Cabot is too strong for him and Abbie comes out to stop him choking Eben. Cabot tells him he's weak and goes inside to celebrate. Abbie tries to be tender with Eben but he rejects her and calls her a liar.

> 'Ye're nothin' but a stinkin' passel o' lies. Ye've been lyin'
> t' me every word ye spoke, day an' night, since we fust –
> done it. Ye've kept sayin' ye loved me....'

She says she loves him and tells him that the promise was made before they fell in love. He says he'll go to California.

They argue and he 'torturedly' says he wished the baby had never been born. Abbie is distraught and she says she'd kill the baby to prove her love for him. He says he won't listen to her but she calls after him that she can 'prove' she loves him and she 'kin do one thin' God does'. Abbie is desperate at the end of the scene.

Scene Three

It is now just before dawn and Eben is in the kitchen ready to leave. Abbie is near the cradle with 'her face full of terror'. She sobs but Cabot stirs and she goes to the kitchen and flings her arms around Eben, kissing him 'wildly'. She says 'I killed him' and he thinks she means Cabot but is horrified when she tells him it's the baby.

Eben states it was his baby and she says she loved it but loves him more. He is angered,

> 'Don't ye tech me! Ye're pizzen! How could ye – t' murder
> a pore little critter – Ye must've swapped yer soul t' hell!

and tells her that he is getting the Sheriff and heads, 'panting and sobbing' to town. She calls out to him that she loves him.

Scene Four

It is after dawn and Abbie is in the kitchen. Cabot wakes in his room and is concerned that he has woken late. He checks the baby and is proud it is quiet and asleep. He goes down to Abbie in the kitchen and she tells him the baby is dead. He runs to check and comes back down and asks 'why?'

In a rage she tells him it was Eben's son and that she loves Eben, not him. He blinks back a tear and then gets 'stony' so he can carry on and says he is going to get the Sheriff. Abbie tells him that Eben's already gone so that Cabot tells her he'll 'git t' wuk.' He then tells her he'd never have told and now he's going to be 'lonesomer'n ever!' Eben comes back and Cabot tells him to get off the farm.

Eben asks for her forgiveness and tells her he loves her. He says he realised he loved her at the Sheriff's and they have a chance to run away but Abbie says she'll take her punishment. Eben says he will share it with her and plans to tell the Sheriff they planned it together. They think they can stand it together and then Cabot comes back.

He goes into a long tirade and tells them how he's let the stock go and will burn the house down. He too plans to go to California but finds that Eben has gotten to his money first. Cabot says that this is a sign from God to him to stay and that 'God's hard an' lonesome!' At this point the Sheriff comes and Eben says he was involved with the baby's murder.

Cabot says 'Take 'em both' and leaves to get his stock. The sun is coming up and as they are led away Eben says the farm's 'Purty' and Abbie agrees. The Sheriff finishes the play with the line, 'It's a jim-dandy farm, no denyin'. Wish I owned it!'

OTHER RELATED TEXTS

Fiction / Non-fiction / Drama

- *Wonder* – R G Palacio
- *First they Killed My Father* – Luong Ung
- *The Graveyard Book* – Neil Gaiman
- *Looking for Alaska* – John Green
- *Eleanor and Park* by Rainbow Rowell
- *The Fault in Our Stars* – John Green
- *We All Fall Down* – Robert Cormier
- *The Old Man and the Sea* – Ernest Hemingway
- *The Fire Eaters* – David Almond
- *Ender's Game* – Orson Scott Card
- *Hatchet* – Gary Paulsen
- *Inside Black Australia* – Kevin Gilbert
- *Sapiens: A Brief History of Humankind* – Yuval Noah Harari
- *Peeling the Onion* – Wendy Orr
- *Raw* – Scott Monk
- *Six Degrees of Separation* – John Guare
- *The Book Thief* – Markus Zusak
- *When Dogs Cry* – Markus Zusak
- *Holes* – Louis Sachar
- *The Outsiders* – S.E. Hinton
- *Roll of Thunder, Hear My Cry* – Mildred D. Taylor
- *A Small Free Kiss in the Dark* – Glenda Millard
- *Monster* – Walter Dean Myers
- *Lord of the Flies* – William Golding
- *Jandamarra* – Steve Hawke
- *A Separate Peace* – John Knowles
- *A Monster Calls* – Patrick Ness
- *The Pigman* – Paul Zindel
- *The Invention of Hugo Cabret* – Brian Selznik

- *Emerald City* – David Williamson
- *Silent Spring* – Rachel Carson

Films and Television

- *The Human Experience* – Charles Kinnane
- *My Brilliant Career* – Gillian Armstrong
- *Broadchurch* – James Strong & Euros Lyn
- *Twinsters* – Samantha Futerman and Ryan Miyamoto
- *Be My Brother* – Genevieve Clay - Smith
- *What's Eating Gilbert Grape* – Lasse Hallstrom
- *Pleasantville* – Gary Ross
- *Eternal Sunshine of the Spotless Mind* – Michel Gondry
- *Taxi Driver* – Martin Scorsese
- *Tootsie* – Sydney Pollack
- *Back in Time for Dinner* – Kim Maddever
- *The Godfather* – Francis Ford Coppola
- *Friends* – David Crane and Marta Kaufmann
- *Dawson's Creek* – Kevin Williamson
- *Orange is the New Black* – Jenji Kohan
- *Boy Meets World* – Michael Jacobs and April Kelly

Website – quote on literature and the human experience

*http://view2.fdu.edu/academics/university-college/school-of-humanities/
english-language-and-literature-program/*

> At its most fundamental level literature explores what it means to be a human being in this world and tries to describe what our human experience is like. As such, literature pushes us to confront the large human questions that have plagued humankind for centuries: issues of fate and free will, issues relating to our role in the universe, our relationship to God, and our

relationships with others. Studying literature not only helps us to understand the complexity of these questions intellectually, but because of its very nature, it allows us to experience these tensions vicariously. Literature does not just tell us about human experience; it recreates it in a way we can feel and visualise. In other words, it calls for a total response from us—it stretches us beyond who we are.

First, literature can enhance our ability to relate to people. Because literature focuses on human relationships and self perception, it can broaden our own experience—to help us understand different kinds of people, different cultures, different problems—and, consequently, help us better understand our own relationships with others.

The study of literature also helps to foster an appreciation for beauty, symmetry, and order. This means more than the intuitive response of liking or disliking something we see or read or hear; it means a carefully thought-through response that will enhance appreciation—not destroy it.

Perhaps the most important skills that the study of literature teaches are analytic and synthetic skills. In learning to read carefully and analytically, we learn to ask hard questions both of the work and of ourselves. And as we seek to discover the relationships between the ideas and images we uncover in a work, our ultimate goal is to see the whole—to see how the parts work together to make the piece what it is. In grappling with the complex and difficult ideas contained in literature, we learn to accept the multiple dimensions and ambiguity that are so often present in life.

Finally, the study of literature will also help develop our writing abilities as we come to value the written word and understand its power to communicate.

Beyond all of these skills, however, it is not what literature can do for us as individuals as much as what it can do to us. Literature speaks to the whole person. Listen to it, says C. S. Lewis, and you will be changed.

Poetry

- 'Warren Pryor' – Alden Nowlan
- 'The Gardener' – Louis MacNeice
- 'The Improvers' – Colin Thiele

Songs

- *Be My Escape* – Relient K
- *Mandolin Wind* – Rod Stewart
- *Roxanne* – The Police
- *Wake Me Up When September Ends* – Green Day
- *Under Pressure* – Queen & David Bowie
- *Candle in the Wind* – Elton John
- *Empire State of Mind* – Alicia Keys
- *Gold Digger* – Kanye West
- *We Are Young* – Fun.
- *Centrefold* – J. Geils Band
- *It's Time* – Imagine Dragons
- *We Cry* – The Script
- *If I Were a Boy* – Beyoncé
- *Shake it Out* – Florence + the Machine
- *C'mon* – Panic! At the Disco & Fun.
- *I Don't Love You* – My Chemical Romance
- *Sing* – My Chemical Romance
- *1985* – Bowling for Soup
- *What About Me* – Shannon Noll
- *Sinner* – Jeremy Loops
- *7 Years* – Lucas Graham

- *Bitter Sweet Symphony* – The Verve
- *Ghost!* – Kid Kudi
- *Good Riddance (Time of Your Life)* – Green Day
- *Expectations* – Belle and Sebastian
- *After Hours* – We Are Scientists
- *Write About Love* – Belle and Sebastian
- *Trust Your Stomach* – Marching Band
- *Heaven Knows I'm Miserable Now* – The Smiths